THE NEW
ebay

THE NEW
ebay

The Official Guide to:
- * Buying
- * Selling
- * Running a profitable business

TODD ALEXANDER

Wrightbooks

First published in 2013 by Wrightbooks
an imprint of John Wiley & Sons Australia, Ltd
42 McDougall St, Milton Qld 4064
Office also in Melbourne

Typeset in ITC Berkeley Oldstyle Std Book 11/13.5

© Todd Alexander

The moral rights of the author have been asserted

National Library of Australia Cataloguing-in-Publication data:

Author:	Alexander, Todd
Title:	The New eBay: the official guide to buying; selling; running a profitable business/Todd Alexander.
ISBN:	9781118588536 (pbk.)
Notes:	Includes index.
Subjects:	eBay (Firm)
	Internet auctions—Australia.
	Finance, Personal—Australia.
	Electronic commerce—Australia.
Dewey Number:	381.177

Cover design by Paul McCarthy

Printed in Singapore by C.O.S. Printers Pte Ltd

10 9 8 7 6 5 4 3 2 1

Disclaimers
Todd Alexander is an employee of eBay but wrote this book independently of his employment. While recognising this as an 'official guide', eBay takes no responsibility for the advice and opinions expressed, and readers are advised that following the recommendations in the book will not guarantee them success in buying and selling on eBay. The contents of this book reflect the views of the author only and do not necessarily reflect the views of eBay.

Yates screenshots published with permission. Yates is a registered trade mark of DuluxGroup (Australia) Pty Ltd and all copyright in the images of Yates products and branding belongs to Yates Australia, a division of DuluxGroup (Australia) Pty Ltd.

The material in this publication is of the nature of general comment only, and does not represent professional advice. It is not intended to provide specific guidance for particular circumstances and it should not be relied on as the basis for any decision to take action or not take action on any matter which it covers. Readers should obtain professional advice where appropriate, before making any such decision. To the maximum extent permitted by law, the author and publisher disclaim all responsibility and liability to any person, arising directly or indirectly from any person taking or not taking action based on the information in this publication.

CONTENTS

ABOUT THE AUTHOR

Todd Alexander has been working in retail and eCommerce for over 20 years. He is currently the Director of Onsite Search at eBay, where he has worked for the past 11 years. During his time at eBay Todd has helped thousands of Australians to buy and sell successfully on the site. This is his third eBay book. The previous titles, *How to Use eBay* and *How to Make Money on eBay*, between them have sold more than 40 000 copies.

Photograph by
Andrew Lasky

Todd is also the author of the internet titles *Why Pay Retail*, *Get Your Business Online Now* and *Everyday Internet at Any Age*. Most of his books have become national bestsellers. He is also the author of the novel *Pictures of Us*.

A regular contributor to online magazines, blogs and webcasts, Todd is widely regarded as Australia's leading eBay expert. He also has degrees in literature and law from Macquarie University.

In what spare time he can find, Todd runs a vineyard, olive grove and accommodation business in the Hunter Valley wine region of NSW, operates a successful eBay business selling garden supplies and continues to write fiction.

Follow Todd on Twitter: @Todd_Alexander

Like Todd's Facebook page: Todd Alexander — author

Visit Todd's website: www.toddalexander.net.au.

ACKNOWLEDGEMENTS

As I celebrate the eleventh anniversary of my employment with eBay, I think about a handful of people who were instrumental in getting me to where my career has taken me today. Some of them have never worked at eBay but without their support (and generally this meant they took a gamble on me) I would not have wound up at eBay, and this book would not exist. So I'd especially like to thank:

> Peter Alexander — for showing me the ropes of the family business and teaching me an invaluable amount; I'm still learning from you today
>
> John Shields — for allowing my foot in the retail door
>
> Pauline Donald — for letting me step into the elevator and for never losing faith
>
> Scot Hayman — for putting the eBay ad on my desk
>
> Stephen Knowles — for allowing my foot in the virtual door
>
> Lee McCabe — for suggesting I should write a book
>
> Deborah Sharkey — for everything else

At Wiley, I've been overwhelmed by the support of the entire team. Lucy Raymond answered an unexpected knock on her door and has provided invaluable guidance, support and commitment ever since. Elizabeth Whiley and Jem Bates, you make a formidable editing team — thank you.

Thanks also to my unofficial team of ongoing mentors, professional and otherwise: Cheryl Akle, Melanie Dudgeon, Jeff Ross, Kirsti Wright, Andrew Marlton and Judy Alexander. Gavin Schwarcz is one of the most knowledgeable men in the publishing industry and I owe him for encouraging me to open my eyes to the obvious. Suz Mitchell — thanks for your expertise.

Last and most certainly not least, thank you to every eBay buyer and seller I've encountered. I consider myself incredibly fortunate to be a member of this community.

INTRODUCTION

Towards the end of 2001 I decided to take my career in a daring new, untested direction. I'd been working for a large, family-owned national book retailer whose future success, it felt at the time, was practically guaranteed. None of my colleagues or friends could believe I would turn my back on a sure-fire industry such as retail to dive headfirst into the uncharted world of eCommerce. I hadn't even heard of eBay when a colleague showed me the job advertisement, but it sounded like an interesting opportunity, and if things didn't work out I could always return to the safety and security of the retail industry.

Who could have predicted that a virtually unknown US online company would become one of Australia's most recognised brands, a rare internet success story and phenomenon, and a way of life for hundreds of thousands of Australians? A year or so into my employment with the company I remember how exciting it was to celebrate the milestone of the first million Australian members. We threw a huge party, web-company style, and couldn't believe the momentum we were experiencing. Today, around ten years later, eBay attracts 7 million Australians every single month—that means roughly one in every two adult Australians visits the site.

eBay has evolved astronomically over the past decade. When I first started working for the company it was known only as 'that auction website', although there were other websites in Australia offering the same kind of experience. Today eBay remains the most popular place to sell second-hand items, but few people are aware of the fact that in Australia more than 80 per cent of the items sold on the site are new, and most of these are sold at fixed price (not auction) by medium to large businesses.

In 2012 eBay reported that its top 2000 sellers experienced sales growth of 45 per cent over the previous year. This is in marked contrast to retail growth figures, which remain more or less flat. The retail industry (and in particular the book industry) is facing one of its toughest periods in history but eCommerce, or online purchasing, is booming. Each year Australians are spending up to $30 billion online and while this still represents a relatively small percentage of total retail, it's hard to deny that Australians have embraced online shopping wholeheartedly.

eBay remains a powerhouse online but its mission is to connect commerce. According to eBay, 'connected commerce is both local and global, online and offline. Big and small players can succeed with each other, not in spite of each other, creating competition that's less "winner takes all" and more "takes all to win"'. The lines between online and offline transactions have blurred. eBay partners with businesses around the world to provide a global platform for trading and will never compete with the sellers on its platform. Most Australians will have visited the site in the past, but in late 2012 eBay's global president, Devin Wenig, launched *The New eBay*—a fresh look and feel for the eBay brand and logo, an overhaul of the site's design, and new functionality that takes the company from its origins as an auction website into the future of commerce. What's even more exciting is eBay's leap into mobile commerce. In 2012, $13 billion worth of eBay transactions were conducted via mobile devices such as the iPhone and the iPad. eBay has become the leading model for how all of us will buy and sell in the future.

In this book, for the first time I'll take you through everything you need to know about buying and selling on eBay, today and into the future. I'll teach you how to use the eBay website but will also cover how to use eBay from mobile devices. Whether you're a casual shopper hoping to save a few dollars or find a rare item, a shopaholic who can't get enough, a casual seller who needs to make some extra cash by disposing of some unwanted items, or an entrepreneur who seeks to start or expand your business and leverage eBay's buyer base to increase your sales—this book has all the information you need.

Whatever your objective, my advice is that first you read the book from beginning to end, because if you want to develop a successful business on eBay you need to know how buyers use the site. If you currently have no intention of selling, I will show you how easy it is to do so and help you make the money you need to buy new products to replace the old. You can then continue to use the book as a handy reference guide; using the index at the back you can dive right in to the section that interests you most, look up specific topics or troubleshoot.

Eleven years into my employment with the company, I've never been more excited about eBay's future and how many opportunities it presents for all

Australians. I have my own business selling on eBay, and throughout this book I will use it as a real-life example of how you too can make money from home or expand your existing business. The book is packed with tips and tricks designed to save you money and time, and is illustrated throughout with colour images taken directly from the eBay website and mobile apps to help you follow along and learn how to get the most out of eBay. Look out for these helpful features throughout the book:

 Follow a practical step-by-step guide to complete certain tasks (you may choose to check the box beside each step as you complete it).

 These tips will help you stay safe when buying and selling online.

Link Whenever you're directed to click on a link on the eBay site or a mobile app, the text in this book will be blue and underlined.

Click Whenever you're directed to click on a button or tab on the eBay site or a mobile app, the text in this book will be bold, green and italicised.

 This icon will appear whenever the iPad app is discussed.

 This icon will appear whenever the iPhone app is discussed.

Whether, like me, you've been a member for more than 10 years or you've never used the site before, welcome to *The New eBay*.

PART I

Getting started

Questions answered in this part

Chapter 1: eBay basics
- What is the difference between the eBay website and eBay apps?
- How do I register on eBay?
- How can I create a good and safe user ID and password?
- How do I update my registration information?
- How do I contact eBay customer support?

eBay basics

There are three ways you can access eBay: via the website, through your mobile phone (such as an iPhone) or via the Apple tablet, iPad. Each platform differs slightly from the others. Throughout this book the variations in the process between web and mobile will be explained.

Introducing eBay's website addresses

To go to eBay's Australian website, type www.ebay.com.au into your internet browser. The first page you see is known as the homepage (see figure 1.1, overleaf). You can navigate your way to most areas of the site from the homepage. Click on the eBay logo at the top left of any page to return to the homepage at any time.

You can also conduct an internet search for the word 'eBay' using a search engine such as Google. Different eBay sites around the world have different website addresses, or URLs. In the UK, for example, the address is www.ebay.co.uk, and in the US it is www.ebay.com. A list of all eBay's international sites is available at the bottom of the homepage. If you're on the Australian eBay site, all listings will automatically be converted into Australian dollars, and you will see a comprehensive list of products from around the world that are available to you here in Australia. Going to an international eBay site will show you still more products; we'll cover this later in part II.

eBay for mobile phones

iPhone You can access eBay via an internet-enabled mobile phone either by logging onto eBay's mobile web address (hp.mobileweb.ebay.com.au/home) or via one of eBay's mobile phone applications (apps). This allows you to access eBay any time of the day and from anywhere your phone receives service. eBay's apps are free to download and provide a better user experience than the mobile web version. You can download the apps for iPhone (see figure 1.2, overleaf), Android, Windows Phone 7 and Blackberry by searching for 'eBay' at your phone provider's app store. All the apps operate in similar ways, but in this book I show you how the apps for iPhone work.

Figure 1.1: the new eBay homepage

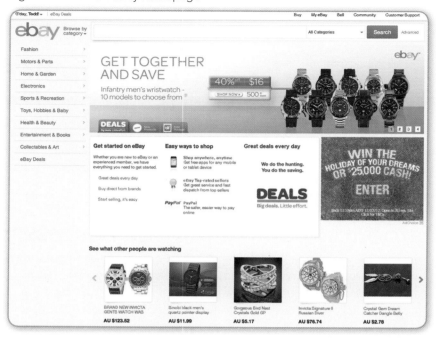

Figure 1.2: the eBay iPhone app

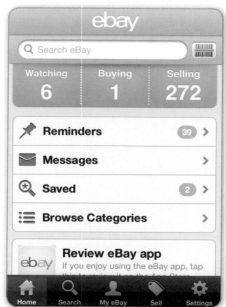

A really useful page on eBay to help identify which app is right for you can be found at http://pages.ebay.com.au/help/account/mobile.html. eBay currently has apps for:

- eBay (overall shopping)
- deals (find the latest products at the biggest discounts on the site)
- fashion (eBay US only)
- motors (eBay US only).

eBay for iPad

iPad If you own an Apple iPad tablet, you can download an iPad app for using eBay (see figure 1.3). This is arguably the most effective and user-friendly way to buy and casually sell on eBay and is well worth checking out. The interface has been specifically designed for use on the iPad. The iPad app is free to download from the Apple App Store.

Figure 1.3: the eBay iPad app

Among many great features of the eBay iPad app are:

- seamless scrolling
- high-resolution product images
- a homepage that can be customised to suit your own tastes
- the ability to buy and sell from one eBay app (take photos with your iPad to list items on eBay faster—refer to part III for more information).

Customising your eBay homescreen on iPad

On the iPad app, click *Edit* at top right to fully customise the way your eBay homescreen appears. You can drag items to rearrange where they appear on the page, or delete some features altogether. Once you're done creating your ideal interface, click *Save*. This is just one of the many benefits of using the iPad app to access eBay. It puts you in control of your own experience and you can update it any time you like.

How to register on eBay

More than 90 million people around the world use eBay each year. Many more people visit an eBay site to look for products or conduct research before purchasing. You do not need to be a member of eBay to search for products, but you do need to be registered before you can purchase an item, sell an item, communicate with other members or complete searches of completed items (that is, to see what has and hasn't sold previously and for what prices). If you haven't already become an eBay member, it's a good idea to do so as it's free and the process takes only a minute or so to complete. Registering now will save you having to do so later before you purchase your first items. Once you're registered, and logged onto the site, your eBay experience will begin to be tailored to your personal tastes, making your whole experience more relevant and rewarding.

Choosing your user ID and password

Choosing the right user ID and password can help protect you through all of your future buying and selling on the site. Don't pick an ID that is the same as your email address or you may be spammed by unsolicited email. Make sure your password is nothing like your user ID and would be difficult for others to guess. Use a combination of letters (upper and lower case) and numbers, and change your password regularly—at least every three months. Taking these steps will help ensure that your eBay account isn't hacked into. Finally, your eBay and PayPal passwords should be different (more information on PayPal in part II).

Let's complete eBay's registration form together so you won't have to do it when you're midway through a purchase or listing an item sometime in the future.

Registering on eBay

☐ On the eBay homepage, next to the eBay logo at the top left, click the text that says <u>Register</u> OR further down the page on the right under the heading 'New to eBay?' click on the *Register* button (see figure 1.4, overleaf). A <u>Register</u> link is also found at the very bottom of every eBay page.

☐ You'll be taken to eBay's registration form for individuals (see figure 1.5, p. 9). Enter your name, address, telephone number and email address in the 'Tell us about yourself' section. Check the details and spelling to ensure everything is correct. To register as a business, click the <u>Want to open an account for your company?</u> link near the top of the page. (For more information on business registration, see part IV.)

☐ If you're having trouble completing the form, two links on the right can help: the question mark and <u>Help</u> at the top of the page take you to eBay's information regarding registration. The *Live help* button will start an instant live chat with one of eBay's customer service agents, who can help guide you through the process.

(continued)

Registering on eBay *(cont'd)*

☐ Choose a user ID that is unique but won't deter others from trading with you (avoid words like 'angry' or 'crazy', for example), and remember that everyone on eBay can see your ID. As you type your ID, eBay will automatically show you whether that ID is available.

☐ Create a password of between 6 and 12 characters. Aim to make it easy for you to remember but difficult for anyone else to guess.

☐ Pick a secret question and answer—this will be used to send you a new password if you ever forget yours.

☐ Enter your date of birth (you need to be at least 18 to use eBay).

☐ Finally, enter the verification code on the screen and review the User agreement and Privacy policy. By checking the 'I accept the User agreement and Privacy policy' box at the bottom of the form, you're agreeing to abide by eBay's rules and policies. Now click the *Continue* button.

Figure 1.4: registering from the eBay homepage

Figure 1.5: eBay's registration form

Once you have completed these steps eBay will send an instant confirmation email to your email address. Click on the Confirm your registration link and enter the confirmation code eBay includes within the email. That's it! Congratulations, you're now an eBay member and can search, bid, buy and begin selling on the site.

Newly registered members will see a small yellow person icon after their user ID. This will be visible to other members for a period of a few weeks and lets the whole eBay community know that you're new to the site (see figure 1.6).

Figure 1.6: eBay user ID

On the iPhone, simply click the *Register* button in the bottom left of the home screen (see figure 1.7, overleaf) and follow the steps as outlined for the website.

Figure 1.7: registering on the eBay
iPhone app

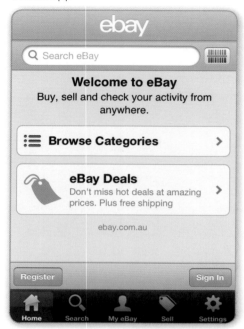

 Click the *Sign in* button (see figure 1.8) on the home screen then click the *Create account* button to complete your registration details.

Signing in to eBay

Each time you visit eBay make sure you are signed in to the site. This way, the information and products you see will be tailored to your preferences and your history of shopping or selling on eBay. On a mobile device, you'll stay signed in permanently if you go to Settings and swipe 'Keep me logged on' to ON. Alternatively, click the *Sign in* button each time you open the eBay app.

For iPad, a small *Sign in* button will appear (see figure 1.8), or use the *Toolbar* tab at top left to display navigation and the button appears at the bottom of the screen.

Figure 1.8: signing in to the eBay iPad app

If you access the website via computer you may need to sign in each time you visit. You will find Sign in right next to Register at the top of the homepage, and further down you'll see the *Sign in* button (see figure 1.4, p. 8). Update your preferences to remain signed in on your computer and eBay will automatically recognise you each time you visit the site. You can stay signed in on your computer by clicking My eBay then Account then Site preferences then click Show next to 'Other general preferences' at the bottom of the screen. Next to 'Keep me signed in on this computer', check the Yes box then click *Apply*. For security reasons you will have to sign in to eBay again every few days.

Updating your information and preferences

At some point in the future you may need to change some of the information in your eBay registration; for example, if you change your email address or move house. To update your information at any time, click My eBay at the top of any eBay page then click Account then Personal information.

Now you're registered on eBay you can also choose how you would like to receive messages from eBay (the company) and from other buyers and sellers on the site. To change or update your communication preferences, click My eBay at the top of any eBay page then click Account then Communication preferences.

My world pages—customise, personalise, share

You can click on any member's user ID to see their eBay My world page (see figure 1.9). Some members list information about themselves on this page. If they are selling anything, a list of some of their items for sale will also appear here. You can edit your own My world page anytime you like and may choose to include, for example, your interests, hobbies, what you like buying and selling, or business information. Including any information on your My world page is completely optional. The My world page will also show information about the member's feedback rating.

Figure 1.9: the My world page

The power of feedback

The entire eBay ecosystem grew around the concept of *feedback*. After all, when the site was invented more than 15 years ago, the idea of buying a product you've never seen from someone you've never met was still fairly radical. Feedback is the system by which eBay members rate each other on their performance as buyers and sellers. It is not a perfect system by any means, but it's one way of helping to ensure that your experience of buying and selling on the site is safe and successful. After every member's user ID, a number in brackets is shown (see figure 1.6 on p. 9). You can click on this number to see the complete feedback profile of any eBay member (see figure 1.10, overleaf).

Every eBay member has a feedback score that represents the total number of positive ratings left by other members less the total number of negative ratings. Note that sellers cannot leave negative ratings for buyers!

Every member also has a positive feedback percentage. This tells you what percentage of their feedback ratings has been positive. This is calculated by taking all of the member's feedback ratings from the past 12 months, adding together the positive and negative scores, then dividing the result by the positive scores. In figure 1.10 you can see that the member has a feedback score of 2702 and has 100 per cent positive feedback. You can also see a red star next to the score of 2702. eBay awards sellers a different coloured star once they have reached predefined feedback milestones. The colours are:

- yellow = 10 to 49
- blue = 50 to 99

- turquoise = 100 to 499
- purple = 500 to 999
- red = 1000 to 4999
- green = 5000 to 9999
- yellow shooting star = 10 000 to 24 999
- turquoise shooting star = 25 000 to 49 999
- purple shooting star = 50 000 to 99 999
- red shooting star = 100 000 to 499 999
- green shooting star = 500 000 to 999 999
- silver shooting star = 1 000 000 plus.

Figure 1.10: feedback profile

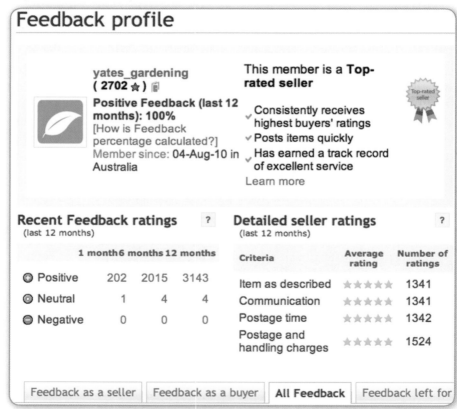

The last 12 months' feedback ratings are shown under the heading 'Recent feedback ratings'. Here you can click on the number of positive, neutral or negative ratings (such as 3143 in the example in figure 1.10) to see all of the comments left. Further down the page you can click on the links for Feedback as a seller, Feedback as a buyer or Feedback left for others to see the corresponding comments.

On leaving feedback

Leaving feedback every time you buy or sell an item is an important part of being an eBay member. It helps everyone trade safely. But before leaving negative or neutral feedback it's always a good idea to contact the member, because most eBay members are very happy to solve your problems, for example by giving you a refund or a replacement product. Never leave rude, offensive or slanderous comments. Be accurate but fair.

The feedback profile page includes other important information too. It tells you how long this member has been registered on eBay, what country they are registered in and, if a seller, whether they're an eBay Top-Rated Seller (eTRS—someone who consistently receives high buyer ratings and has a proven track record of fast postage and great service), and shows you Detailed seller ratings (more information later in this chapter).

Revising your feedback

Sometimes a seller may contact you after resolving an issue to ask you to change the feedback you have left. It's important to know that leaving negative feedback for your seller can affect their sales volume and eBay reputation. If you wish to review and revise the feedback you have left, you have 30 days to do so. If the seller sends you an email requesting the revision, simply click the *Accept request* button and follow the prompts to update the feedback for the seller. You can also revise negative or neutral feedback if you have accidentally left it for the wrong seller. To do so, click the Customer support link at the top of any eBay page, type 'revise feedback' in the help search then click Contact eBay to have eBay remove the incorrect feedback on your behalf.

Detailed seller ratings

Another form of feedback you can leave for sellers is called Detailed Seller Ratings (DSRs). The last 12 months' ratings are displayed in the feedback profile (see figure 1.10, p. 14). Any seller who has received at least 10 DSRs will have their scores displayed. For each transaction, you score the seller out of five (five being the highest, one being the lowest) on the following service factors:

- *Item as described*—Was the item you received in the condition, and of the type, described by the seller in their listing?

- *Communication*—Did the seller respond efficiently and effectively to your communications? (You will be able to rate this aspect only if you have communicated with the seller via eBay's My messages system.)

- *Postage time*—How long did it take the seller to get the item in the post? (This is not a measurement of how long it took the delivery service to get the item to you.)

- *Postage and handling charges*—Were the charges fair and accurate? (If the seller sent you the goods without charging you postage, they automatically receive five stars.)

Site navigation and other eBay information

Click Site map at the bottom of any eBay page to see a list of the most popular pages of the site—all just one click away.

At the bottom of every eBay page you will find other useful information about the company, including About eBay (corporate information), Media centre (eBay media releases), Policies (a list of the most important rules and policies for using eBay), and links to the eBay User agreement and Privacy policy.

eBay help and customer support

If at any time you need assistance in using the site or resolving a problem, there are several ways to get help on eBay. Click Customer support at the top right of any eBay page or the same link at the very bottom of any eBay page.

In the 'Find an answer' section, enter keywords for the topic you'd like to see more information about. To contact eBay, click Contact eBay. Here you will be guided through broad subject areas (Buying, Selling, My account) so eBay can put you in touch with the right service agent. Once you have identified the area of your query, choose between the following methods of customer service:

- *Email*—email your question to receive a written email response, usually within 24 hours.

- *Live chat*—type your question to have a service agent answer it instantly in real time. Live chat hours are 7 am to 11 pm (AEST/AEDT) seven days per week (check for possible changes to hours of service).

- *Telephone*—call customer support and speak to a service agent, generally within around two to five minutes. Hours are weekdays 8 am to 9 pm and weekends 8 am to 5 pm (AEST/AEDT; check for possible changes to hours of service).

- *Return call*—ask customer support to telephone you (again, they will normally respond within around two to five minutes). Hours are the same as for telephone support.

iPad For iPad, go to Settings and click Contact eBay support for email help.

iPhone For iPhone, go to Settings and click Contact eBay support to navigate to the right area of help. If the information provided does not answer your question, click Need more help? Contact us at the bottom of the screen. Click the *Email* button, fill in your details, click *Submit* and have eBay email you a response to your query.

eBay on social network sites

Through Facebook and Twitter you can stay connected with eBay, communicate with other eBay members on important topics, and share fun information and tips. Follow eBay on Facebook at www.facebook.com/eBay.com.au. Click *Need help* for answers to your eBay questions. Follow eBay on Twitter at @eBayAU.

The eBay community

eBay was one of the very first social networks on the internet. Today thousands of eBay members communicate via the site's discussion boards, and many are happy to answer questions, offer advice, or share their own buying and selling experiences so you can learn from them. To access eBay's chatboards and forums, click Community at the top of any page. Community cannot be accessed from eBay mobile apps.

eBay events

eBay occasionally hosts or attends industry events to help you learn more about being a successful eBay seller or about the future direction of the company. Attending these events offers invaluable opportunities to network and to learn from experienced and knowledgeable sellers. Events are announced via eBay news pages on the site. Keep a lookout for Internet conference (www. internetconference.com.au), the conference for professional eCommerce and eBay sellers attended by more than 500 delegates each year.

Important messages from eBay

You may receive important messages and updates from eBay, such as changes to the fees charged to sell an item, news of new or updated technology on the site, or changes to its User agreement or Privacy policy. These messages will always appear within the My eBay section of the site, which can be accessed by clicking My eBay at the top of any eBay page and then clicking the *Messages* button. Announcements are also made on eBay's announcement board, which can be accessed by clicking Community at the top of any eBay page then clicking eBay news.

New eBay features

If you're keen to check out the very latest eBay features being trialled and tested, be sure to visit The garden on the eBay US site. Products tested and approved here may eventually be rolled out on eBay sites across the globe. It's a great way to participate in tests and provide feedback, and to monitor the future direction of the company. To view the latest developments, go to the eBay US homepage (www.ebay.com), scroll down to the bottom of the page and click Preview new features under the 'Community' heading.

PART II

Finding and buying products

Questions answered in this part

(continued)

Questions answered in this part *(cont'd)*

Chapter 5: The View item page
- What is the View item page?
- What information is the most important?
- How do I ask a seller a question?

Chapter 6: Bidding on and buying products
- How do I bid on an auction?
- What is proxy bidding?
- How do I buy an item listed as Buy it now?
- Can I make a counter-offer to the seller?
- What is a second chance offer?

Chapter 7: Paying for an item
- How do I pay with PayPal?
- Can I pay with credit card?
- How do I transfer money into the seller's bank account?
- What is Paymate?

Chapter 8: Keeping track of purchases in My eBay
- How do I keep track of everything I have bought or bid on?
- How do I create lists of products I like?
- How do I access a favourite search or seller?
- What is My messages?

Chapter 9: Troubleshooting purchases
- What is the first thing I do if I encounter a problem?
- What happens if I change my mind?
- What if I do not receive my product?
- What if the product is broken or not what I was expecting?
- What is eBay's resolution centre?
- What is PayPal buyer protection?

Chapter 2
Searching for products

Not everyone uses eBay only to purchase items. It's also a great way to conduct research into one of the world's largest selections of products to gauge both price and popularity. Using a mobile device means you carry with you an instant price check to ensure you never pay more than you need to for a product. There are several ways to find products on eBay.

Basic product searches

At the top of every eBay page is the eBay search bar. It's a white box with a *Search* button at the end of it (see figure 2.1). eBay's search functionality works by referencing the item titles entered by eBay sellers, along with other product information such as the category in which the product is listed, against the keywords you enter in the search box.

Figure 2.1: the eBay search bar

A very broad search (such as 'dress') could reveal millions of matching products, so it's always best to include several important keywords (such as 'black cocktail dress size 12'). To conduct a basic search, enter your keywords and click *Search*. eBay will automatically prompt you with a list of popular search terms as you begin to type your keywords. You can click on any one of these terms to be taken automatically to corresponding search results.

On the iPad and iPhone, enter your keywords within the search box at the top of the home screen then click *Search* on your device's keypad. On the iPhone you can also click *Search* at the bottom of the screen (see figure 1.7, p. 10), or for iPad click the *Toolbar* tab at top left (see figure 1.8, p. 11) then click *Search*.

One of the great functions on the iPhone app is that you can scan barcodes to conduct precise product searches. Not every single barcode can be referenced, because more are being added every day. To scan a barcode, click the *barcode icon* next to the search bar (see figure 1.7, p. 10), hold your phone's camera over the product's barcode and wait for the app to capture the code. Once it's captured, the app will automatically search eBay for all matching products.

Category searches

Sometimes a given word may have two different meanings. For example, the word 'clutch' denotes both a handbag and a car part, and 'seed' is a clothing brand and a gardening product. Conducting a more advanced search will often help you find what you're looking for much faster. Rather than searching the entire site for 'clutch', for example, you could narrow the search so as to display only products in the 'Clothing, shoes & accessories' category.

To restrict a keyword search to a given category, type your keyword(s) into the search bar then click the down arrow next to the words 'All categories'. Click on the category that best describes where you're most likely to find the products you want, then click *Search*.

You can also refine your search results by category once they appear on the screen (see the step-by-step guide later in this chapter). Make sure you choose the category carefully, as some sellers may list products under more than one category, so by restricting your search you may miss seeing every product that matches.

For iPhone and iPad, first enter your keywords then click *Search*. Once your results have been returned click *Refine*. In the Refine pop-up, next to 'Category', click *All*. Click the category that best captures your product choice then click *Done* (for iPad) or click *Refine* then *Search* (for iPhone).

Advanced searches

You can refine your search by much more than just the category it is listed in. This is called an advanced search and can be completed in one of two ways. First, you can click <u>Advanced</u> next to *Search* in the eBay search bar (see figure 2.1, p. 21). This opens the Advanced search form, where you can choose from a long list of search refinement options, including:

- category
- search title and description
- price ranges
- buying format (auction, fixed price, and so on—see part III)
- free shipping or local pick-up
- items within a certain kilometre radius of your location.

On this page you can also choose to search products from select sellers and items in eBay stores, and find other members along with their contact information. Once you've chosen which filters to apply to your search, click *Search* at the bottom of the page.

The other way to conduct an advanced search is to enter your keywords in the search bar, click *Search* and then on the search results page use the filters on the left to narrow the results further.

Let's refine a search step by step. In this example, we begin by choosing a very broad term as our keyword and enter 'dress' in the eBay search box then click *Search*. There are more than 2 million results that contain 'dress' in the item title.

We need to narrow it down by category, so on the search results page we choose 'Women's Clothing' then <u>Dresses</u> (see figure 2.2). Note how in the search bar at the top of the page 'in Women's Clothing' appears next to the search term. If you want to look more broadly than in one category, simply click the 'x' next to 'in Women's Clothing'.

Figure 2.2: refining a product search

We only want products with free postage so we click <u>Free shipping</u> under 'Show only'.

Next we narrow the search further by choosing the correct size type, style, occasion, colour and length (note that these product details, or item specifics, will vary depending on the category you have filtered by). For this kind of product, we don't want second-hand or used items so we click <u>New with tags</u> under the 'Condition' heading. We don't want to wait for an auction to end so we click <u>Buy it now</u> under 'Format' to remove all auctions from our search results.

While we can click on each of these links individually and wait for the search results list to update each time, we can also click on <u>See all</u> to select multiple filters at once. This is the fastest, most effective way to refine our search results. Once we've chosen all of our filters (note the other option links on the right), we click **Go** (see figure 2.3).

Figure 2.3: choosing multiple search refinements

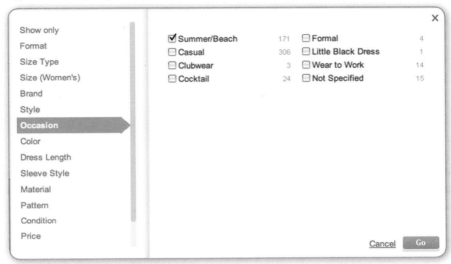

To change our filters, on the left of the search results page we uncheck any individual box that we have selected (see figure 2.4, overleaf), or at the top of the page uncheck any one of the small grey boxes, or click <u>Clear all</u> to remove all search refinements.

In this example, over 1.4 million results for 'dress' have been narrowed down to 39 products that best match our requirements. Now we can look through the results to find the product we most want to buy.

Searching for products

Figure 2.4: Search
results page with search
refinements

Another search refinement available for most types of products on the site is to view items from specific locations only. You may wish to limit your search to sellers located in Australia, for example, or to every product available worldwide that can be shipped to Australia. Check the relevant box beneath the heading 'Item location'. You may want to search only for some favourite sellers or sellers with eBay stores. To do so, check the relevant box beneath the heading 'Seller' in the search refinement pop-up or at the bottom of the list of search refinements on the left side of the Search results page.

To conduct an advanced search on the iPhone or iPad, follow the steps outlined in 'Category searches' earlier in this chapter by accessing the Refine pop-up box.

Tips for finding great deals

By using advanced search, you can quickly and efficiently obtain a set of search results that are customised towards finding you a great deal.

Tip

Finding the best deal for you

- Check the 'Completed listings' box to review recently sold and unsold items; this helps you to set a fair market price expectation for the item you want to buy.

- Check the 'Title and description' box to reveal some hidden gems—sellers have only 80 character spaces to complete their item title so it's often impossible to include every relevant keyword.

- Check the 'Best offer' box to find items where sellers are willing to negotiate on price.

- Check the 'Free postage' box to save on delivery costs.

- Check the 'Sale items' box to locate products whose prices have recently been reduced by the seller.

- Check the 'Auction format' box. In the 'Number of bids' box, enter '0' in the maximum field, then in the 'Show items priced' box, enter a low dollar figure in the maximum field. This way you'll see low-priced auctions with no bids, and if you check the 'Listings ending within 1 hour' box you'll also see those ending very soon. A good tip is to do this late at night when fewer bidders will be online.

- If you have a favourite brand or celebrity you like searching for, try misspelling the name a few different ways to find items other buyers using the correct spelling may miss.

- On the search results page, don't limit yourself to the first one or two pages—try a bit of pot luck and click on a high page number at the bottom of the results. Few buyers do this, and you might find a great deal.

- As with all searches, make sure you review the seller's credentials and read all product information carefully before committing to buy.

Searching for products

27

Save your favourite searches

There will be some searches that you keep returning to, and you won't want to have to do the necessary filtering every time. eBay makes this easy by allowing you to save your favourite searches. You can even have eBay email you every time a new product matching your search is listed on the site. To save one of your favourite searches, on the search results page click Save search; to receive emails check the 'Email me daily when new items match my search' box and click *Save*.

If you've conducted your search from the search bar on the eBay homepage, you will also have the option of saving the search from there. Click *Save* (see figure 2.5). eBay will also show you a list of your recent searches on the homepage when you are logged in.

Figure 2.5: saving a search from the search bar

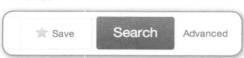

To edit, delete or add more saved searches, click My eBay at the top of any page then click *Saved searches*.

On the iPad and iPhone, simply click the star button to save your favourite searches. On the iPad you can add this to your homepage, so accessing your favourite searches is always one click away. You can easily add more saved searches, recent searches, favourite categories or products to your homepage on iPad by clicking the blue + button at bottom right of the screen (see figure 1.3, p. 5).

eBay feed — tailor your eBay experience

New to eBay, and available only on the US site at present, is eBay feed. By telling eBay some of your favourite things on the site, your eBay experience will be tailored to your individual likes. Feed uses complex algorithms to locate products similar to those you like and cross-references these with products purchased by people with similar likes to yours. Click eBay feed at the bottom of the homepage and enter your favourite searches, items or sellers to view relevant products. Even if you're not signed up to eBay feed, your eBay homepage will show you products relevant to your past activities.

The iPad experience is automatically tailored to your past searches and purchases. Look out for future enhancements to this feature.

Chapter 3
The search results page

When you conduct a search on eBay, the products returned to you appear on what is called the search results page. eBay's default search algorithm is known as Best match, but before we get into what Best match is and how it works, let's spend some time familiarising ourselves with the search results page (see figure 3.1, overleaf).

Navigate the search results page

The eBay logo, search bar and top right links remain the same on every eBay page. Beneath your entered keyword(s) (in this example, 'dress') you will see a list of related searches as suggested by eBay. Clicking on any of these links will take you to a search results page for your keyword(s).

Staying in the grey area of the page, towards the left are the various search refinement filters (as covered in chapter 2). These filters change depending on the category or type of product you are looking at. On the right of the greyed area under the heading 'Popular on eBay' are some paid advertisements from eBay sellers or for third-party companies.

In the white area in the centre of the page are the actual search results. For example, if I search for 'dress', at the top of the page I am told there are 147 active listings that match my search refinements, and next to it there are two links: one for Sold listings (clicking this link will show me all items that have recently sold) and one for Completed listings (clicking on this link will show me both sold and unsold and completed recent listings).

To the right is the Sort drop-down, which defaults to Best match (more on Best match later in the chapter). You can change the sort order to ending soonest, newly listed, price + postage (lowest or highest first), item price (highest first) or distance from your postcode (nearest first).

The View drop-down box allows you to further customise the layout of the page, including column order, additional information (such as image size and items per page) and gallery or side-by-side picture view.

As covered in chapter 2, if you have used search refinements, each chosen refinement will be highlighted in a small button above your search results (*Buy it now*, *New with tags* and so on). An eBay advertisement or message may appear underneath these.

Product information on the search results page

Now, finally, we get to the actual products for sale. First you will see a photograph of the item (as shown in figure 3.1). You can click on the small magnifying glass to see a pop-up box highlighting the main information about the product for sale, or click on the image of the product to be taken through to the View item page (where you can see all the information about the product and the seller—more on this in chapter 5).

If the product is new to eBay a small white box with green writing will say 'Newly listed' before the item title. The item title is linked through to the View item page. The title is created by the seller of the product and should contain all of the most important keywords to describe the item for sale. Beneath the item title a seller may also create an item subtitle to explain more about the product for sale or the terms of sale.

Figure 3.1: Search results page

If a link for <u>More options</u> appears (as in the first listing in figure 3.1), it signifies that the seller has a range of similar products for sale (these could be in different sizes, colours or materials, for example).

Key product attributes (in this example, 'Dress length: full-length') may appear also. These are known as item specifics or seller tags.

If the product is coming from an international destination, the country where the product is located will be highlighted (such as 'From Thailand' in both listings in figure 3.1). In the top right click the drop-down arrow next to 'View' to show additional seller information. If the seller has an eBay store (basically a website within eBay that merchandises all of the seller's products in one location), the store name can appear. You can click on the name of any store to be taken to it directly.

Seller user ID is the name of the seller. This, and the seller's feedback rating and score (highlighted here as 'reviews') can also appear. If the seller is an eBay Top-Rated Seller, a small medal icon will be shown (as in the listings in figure 3.1). For more on the eBay Top-Rated Seller program, see chapter 1.

If the product is available in a range of colours, the spectrum of available colours will appear beneath this information. Click on one of the coloured bars to see the same item in the corresponding colour.

If the seller offers a fast postage option, it will display 'Expedited shipping available'.

To the right of the item title, the time remaining for auctions will be displayed. Note this only applies to auction format and not Buy it now listings. In the last seconds of an auction, the time will automatically count down.

On the far right of the white area of the page you will see the price and the format of the item (auction or Buy it now). If it is an auction item you will see how many bids have been placed. Some listings will have both an auction price and a Buy it now price so you can choose the format you prefer. For more about buying formats, see chapter 6.

The shipping costs will appear beneath the item price if they have been specified by the seller.

The search results page

33

Best match

As mentioned earlier, eBay's default search order is created by the Best match algorithm. Best match looks at a wide combination of factors to show shoppers the most relevant products for their entered search. Best match looks at factors such as:

- *recent sales* — the listings with the most items sold in the last 7 days will appear closer to the top of the list

- *relevancy* — factors such as the category in which the item is listed, the seller's product details and the keywords of your search to show you the most relevant products

- *seller performance* — sellers with a proven track record of service and positive ratings from their buyers will appear closer to the top of the list

- *price* — factors such as the relative price of the item and postage costs will influence where the item appears on the list

- *buying format* — there is a healthy balance of auctions and Buy it now listings on each page so the most popular format within each category can be viewed by the most people.

Best match is continually evolving and will frequently introduce new factors to ensure you always see the most relevant products at the top of the search results page for every search you complete.

You can change the default search order at any time, and even permanently set up your search order to be different from Best match (as described earlier in this chapter). However, just as Google's algorithm can generally be relied on to show the most relevant set of search results, Best match is the default choice for the vast majority of eBay shoppers.

On the iPhone, search results pages are very simple. Displayed in a three-column format are the photo of the item; the item title; and the price, postage, number of bids and the time remaining for auctions (or the words Buy it now to denote that format).

For iPad, the same information appears except the images are larger and the layout is in a window-type format (see figure 3.2). Use any of the three buttons at top right to change the way the search results are configured (for example, you can view larger pictures without item titles).

Figure 3.2: Search results on the iPad

Now you have familiarised yourself with all of the components of the search results page, you're ready to see more about the products you want to buy. We'll cover the View item page in chapter 5, but first let's look at another way of finding products on eBay—browsing.

Chapter 4
Browsing for products

Perhaps you don't know exactly what you're looking for every time you visit eBay? Some people love to 'window shop' for hours on end, hoping to encounter that unexpected treasure or bargain. You can also browse eBay for items by clicking on one of the category links on the eBay homepage.

Browse categories

The most popular categories are listed beneath the eBay logo, or you can click Browse by category to see all options (see figure 4.1). In the category pop-up, make sure you click the See all categories link to view every one.

Figure 4.1: browsing by category

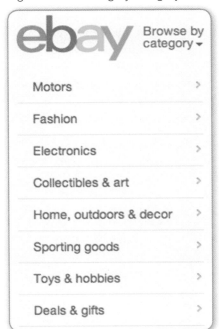

 For iPhone, click <u>Browse categories</u> on the home screen, and for iPad click *Browse* at the top of the home screen.

eBay product merchandising

Throughout the site, eBay displays the most popular categories and products to inspire purchasers. Often what is displayed to you will relate to your previous eBay activities, and in future most of what you see will be tailored to your individual likes. Figure 1.1, p. 4, for example, features watches and jewellery, whereas figure 1.8, p. 11, displays popular electronic devices such as the iPad.

eBay Deals

If you're always on the lookout for an irresistible bargain, look no further than eBay's Deals hub. Here you'll find a selection of brand new, heavily discounted products — including some of the biggest brands — from a range of eBay's best sellers, and often with free postage. The shopping experience is easy, with clear and larger images, and as all products have been vetted by eBay you know you're getting a great deal.

The Deals hub includes a combination of daily deals (one or two hero products each day), weekly deals (hundreds of discounted products across a wide range of categories), group buys (an amazingly good deal that requires a minimum number of buyers to commit before the sale is activated), seasonal sales (such as Christmas and End of Financial Year) and special sales from selected sellers (usually discounted brand-name items).

To access eBay's Deals, click *Deals* at the top of the eBay homepage. In the Deals hub (see figure 4.2), click on a product image or title to see more information, or click one of the category links to browse all deals in that specific category.

By subscribing to daily email alerts you need never miss out on a bargain again (eBay deals are usually in limited supply and available for a limited time). To subscribe, simply click *Don't miss a deal* at the top of the Deals hub.

Figure 4.2: the eBay Deals hub

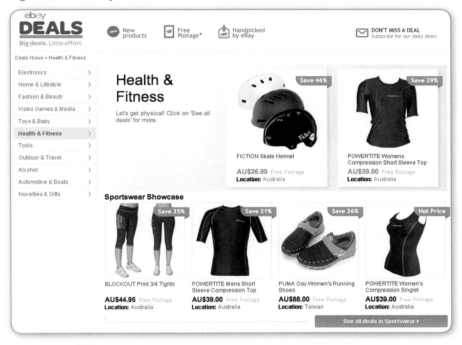

 On the iPhone, *eBay Deals* appears on the home screen but a direct link is not available on the iPad. (Look out for this to change soon.) Remember that apps specifically for eBay Deals are available from your device's app store.

Advertising on eBay

As you browse the eBay site you will notice a number of advertisements. Some are from eBay sellers and will redirect you to their eBay store or to a list of all the products they have for sale. Other advertisements are paid for by third parties and clicking on one of these may redirect you away from eBay. Most placements will be tailored to your specific search so should have some relevance. At the bottom of search results pages you will also see Google advertisements for other websites. These appear as text links under the heading 'Sponsored results' and relate specifically to the keywords you have entered in your search. Clicking on these will redirect you to a website outside of eBay.

Chapter 5
The View item page

Now that you've found the product you're most interested in, by either searching or browsing the site, you will have clicked on an image or description of the product to be taken to the View item page (see figure 5.1). It's important to know that the seller of the item has added most of the information on this page. It is the most important page of the buying process, and you should read all the information carefully before committing to purchase or bidding on an item.

Figure 5.1: the View item page

Ask questions!

If you're unsure about any aspect of the product or the seller's terms of trade, always contact the seller to ask for clarification *before* committing to buy. Sellers will generally be fast and efficient at responding to your questions. Never buy an item if you have unresolved questions and the seller does not respond, or if their response is unsatisfactory. There is a high chance that another seller will be selling the same item, so choose to purchase from someone else rather than running the risk that the item will not be exactly what you want.

Let's take a close look at each of the areas of the View item page. At the top of the page is the standard eBay logo and search bar. Note at top right a link to Cart will appear in the future, which you can click on at any time to see the items you have added to your cart (more about the cart later in this chapter).

Beneath the eBay logo is the Back to search results link. Clicking on this will return you to your search results page. Next to this is the category in which the product is listed. You can click on any of the category names to see all of the products listed within that category.

In the middle left of the page, you will see one or multiple photographs of the item. You can click on the image to see a larger version of the photograph or zoom in for more detail (if a large enough image has been uploaded by the seller). You can also click on any of the smaller images beneath the main photo to see more detail.

Beneath the image(s) you may also see a small Have one to sell? Sell it yourself link. Clicking on this will take you to eBay's Selling form, which will prefill a lot of the product information for you, based on the item you are currently looking at. At top right of the image box, a small orange circle will appear if the seller offers free postage. The circle contains the text 'FREE shipping' or 'FREE postage'.

In the middle section of the page, the seller creates the item title—in this case, 'Yates Thrive All Purpose...'. Sellers have up to 80 characters with which to create their item title. Beneath the title three buttons can add the product to your eBay favourites list, which will appear in My eBay (more on that in chapter 8). The first button, *Like*, allows you to Like the item on your Facebook profile; the second button, *Want*, communicates to your friends that you more than like it; the third button, *Own*, tells your Facebook friends that you already have the item—perhaps you want their feedback or you just want to brag that you have one.

The next section in the middle of the page (figure 5.1, p. 41) displays more detailed information about the product, starting with its condition. A seller can choose one of eBay's predefined conditions or add keywords to describe the condition of the item (in this example, Brand New).

If the item is being sold at auction, the time remaining before the end of the auction will appear beneath Item condition. For Buy it now items, the Quantity box allows you to specify how many of the item you would like to purchase (if more than one is available) and will also tell you how many of this item the seller has sold.

The price appears within a grey-coloured area in the centre of the page. The currency will default to the eBay site you are shopping on (in this example, the currency is US dollars). If the product is a Buy it now listing, only one price appears; if it is sold at auction, the current bid price appears and you must enter a price higher than this amount to outbid the current high bidder. A link to how many previous bids have been made will also appear. There may be a combination of auction and Buy it now listings (we'll cover this more in chapter 6).

Three buttons appear next to the item price. The first says *Buy it now*. In this example, the seller has listed the product only in the fixed price format, which means you're unable to bid and can only pay the set asking price. Coming soon to eBay Australia, the second button will say *Add to cart*, which puts the item in your virtual shopping basket. You can add more items to the list and pay for them all at once after you have finished shopping. If this was an auction, the first button would say *Place bid* and the *Add to cart* button would disappear. Note that some sellers use a combination of auction and Buy it now, which means all three buttons appear and you have the option of placing a bid, buying immediately or adding to cart. Once a bid has been placed on the item the Buy it now and cart options disappear. Other sellers may also allow you to make an offer lower than their set asking price and if this option is available a further button, *Make offer*, will appear. All of these buying options will be fully explained in chapter 6. A small white button, *Add to watch list*, will appear regardless of buying format. Click on the small arrow to add the item to either your watch list or your wish list, and it will appear within My eBay.

Shipping, delivery, payments and returns information appears beneath the item price and buying buttons.

In the example in figure 5.1 (p. 41) information about PayPal's buyer protection appears (for more information see chapter 7). For the US, a logo for eBay Buyer protection appears—note that this scheme is currently available only on the eBay US site, but look for this to change soon.

On the right of the page, four social media buttons allow you to share the product's details with friends via email, Facebook, Twitter or Pinterest.

The 'Seller information' box in grey tells you more about the person or business selling this item. Click on the user ID (in this example, yates gardening) to view the seller's My world page, or click on the number after the user ID (in this example, 2702) to view the seller's feedback profile and a coloured star will appear next to the feedback score to denote whether the seller has reached one of eBay's feedback milestones (as covered in chapter 1). Beneath this the overall percentage of positive feedback received by the seller is listed.

You can click Save this seller to add them to your Favourite sellers list in My eBay and click See other items to see all of the items for sale from this seller. If the seller has an eBay store (a seller-branded website within eBay where all their items appear and can be searched for, along with other information about the seller), a logo of a small red door will appear with the name of the seller's store (in this example, Yates Gardening).

An advertisement for eBay or a third party will generally appear beneath the 'Seller information' box.

Beneath all of this information are two tabs: *Description* and *Postage and payments* (note that the terms *postage* and *shipping* are interchangeable on eBay). In the *Description* tab, all of the main product information (such as condition, brand, material, size and colour) will be summarised under the heading 'Item specifics', if the seller has included this information, and the category under which the product is listed. Some products on eBay can be listed by using a catalogue of data stored on eBay. Most catalogues contain comprehensive product information from the manufacturer or an industry body. Where this is available, a second box will appear with the information under the heading 'Detailed item info'.

Clicking on the *Postage and payments* tab (see figure 5.2) will show detailed information on whether the seller ships to your location, the cost of shipping, the estimated handling time, whether returns are accepted and what payment methods are accepted. It's particularly important to read this information carefully so you're fully aware of all of the costs and the time frame associated with purchasing the product from this seller.

Figure 5.2: the Postage and payments tab

To the right of these tabs are three important pieces of information: a link that allows you to <u>Print</u> the product details (it's a good idea to print this information for anything you purchase and to store it safely for future reference), a link to <u>Report item</u> (if you think the listing contravenes any of eBay's rules or policies) and the item number. You can make a note of the item number and search for it by entering it into eBay's search bar. The item number may also be required for specific eBay processes such as revising feedback.

Further down the page beneath the *Description* tab is more detailed product and terms of trade information entered by the seller in the format of their choice.

Figure 5.3 (overleaf) is an example of a professional eBay seller's detailed item description using the web-design language HTML. The seller has incorporated images within the listing and used eBay's Store frame, which allows buyers to click through to specific store categories from within the listing. Other eBay sellers may use plain text to describe their product(s) and their terms of trade.

Figure 5.3: example of a seller's detailed item description

If unsure, ask the seller

Always read every word of a seller's detailed item description so you know everything about the product and the seller's terms of trade (including any additional postage costs or time delays) before you proceed with buying the item. If you're unsure about anything, ask the seller a question. If you don't receive a satisfactory answer, it's best to avoid purchasing from that seller and to try another seller offering the same or a similar item. To contact your seller, scroll to the very bottom of the detailed item description and click the Ask a question link on the left. Previously asked questions and answers may also appear under the heading 'Questions and answers about this item'; you can also click on the Contact member link (website) or *Ask seller a question* button (eBay apps) within their feedback profile.

 View item pages look quite different on the iPad and iPhone apps. Figure 5.4 shows a typical listing on the iPhone. At the top of the screen a small grey *Search* button takes you back to your search results and a small grey *Watch* button at top right adds this product to your app's watch list. A small image appears on the left. You can click on the image to see a larger version. The item title appears next to the image of the product. Beneath these, the price, quantity available, postage cost and item location appear, as well as the locations to which the seller ships.

Figure 5.4: the iPhone View item screen (top)

When you scroll down the screen (see figure 5.5, overleaf), there are links to <u>Condition</u>; <u>Description</u>; <u>Item specifics</u>; <u>Shipping, Payments, Returns</u> and <u>Seller</u>. Each of these links takes you to the corresponding area of the View

The View item page

item page, as outlined for the eBay website earlier in this chapter. Scroll down to the bottom of the screen to see three buttons: *Buy it now* (or *Place bid* for auctions), *Sell one like this* and *Share this item*. A fourth *Select options* button appears if the seller has different product variations available from within the listing.

Figure 5.5: the iPhone View item screen (bottom)

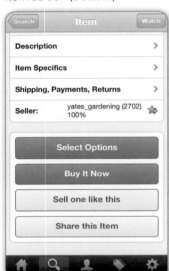

For iPad, the View item screen is slightly different again. Figure 5.6 shows a typical example. Once you have clicked on any item in the iPad search results page, a selection of the top matching results will move to the navigation area on the left of the screen to allow you to compare these products easily.

At the top of the screen are the Watch, Share and More like this links. Watch and Share perform a similar action to those links outlined earlier in this chapter for the iPhone and website. More like this will take you to a new search results page that shows you similar items.

Figure 5.6: the iPad View item screen (top)

A photograph of the item appears below these links—you can click on the image to see a larger version of it. The item title appears beneath the image, then the item and postage prices. Beneath these you will see a *Buy it now* button, or *Place bid* if the item is listed at auction. A *Select options* button will appear if the seller has product variations available from within this listing (such as different sizes, colours and so on)

Click on the seller name (in this example, <u>yates gardening</u>) to see the seller's feedback profile or click on the small arrow next to the name to see all items for sale from this seller. Postage/shipping, location and payment information appears beneath this. Click on the *More details* button to see information such as the category under which the product is listed, the quantity available, handling time, item-specific information and the seller's returns policy.

Finally, at the bottom of the screen the seller enters the detailed item description. Click on the four small arrows in the panel on the right to see the description in full screen mode.

Chapter 6
Bidding on and buying products

In chapters 2 to 4 we learned how to search and browse for products on eBay and find the most appealing products within a search results page. In chapter 5 we carefully reviewed all of the item and seller information on the View item page. Now that we're confident we've found the best item from the best seller, we're ready to bid at auction or Buy it now.

Bid at auction

When a seller has listed a product for sale using the auction format, you will be asked to enter a bid amount. eBay will specify the minimum bid amount required—in the example in figure 6.1, the bidder is advised to 'Enter US $11.49 or more'.

Figure 6.1: placing a bid

When a seller has listed the product on an overseas eBay site, that site's default currency will appear and eBay will make the conversion for you ('Approximately AU $10.67' in figure 6.1). Minimum bid increments are automatically decided by eBay, depending on the current highest bid. Table 6.1 (overleaf) identifies how these increments are determined.

Table 6.1: eBay auction bidding increments

Current price	Bid increment
$0.01–$0.99	$0.05
$1.00–$4.99	$0.25
$5.00–$24.99	$0.50
$25.00–$99.99	$1.00
$100.00–$249.99	$2.50
$250.00–$499.99	$5.00
$500.00–$999.99	$10.00
$1000.00–$2499.99	$25.00
$2500.00–$4999.99	$50.00
$5000.00 and above	$100.00

If previous bids have been made on the product, a link to the right of the price will appear (in this example, 1 bid). Clicking on this link will take you to a (de-identified) list of previous bidders, the amount bid, the time and date of the bid, and the original start price of the auction.

You can either enter the minimum amount required or use something called proxy bidding. Proxy bidding on eBay allows you to enter any amount above the minimum bid required, and the eBay system will automatically bid on your behalf up to that amount each time a new bid is made by another bidder. In the example below, we may enter $15.00 in the Bid box. This means that whenever any other bidder enters a bid amount below $15.00, the eBay proxy bidding system will automatically bid on your behalf to ensure you remain the highest bidder. If a bidder enters $12.00, your proxy bid will be $12.50 and that becomes the new highest bid; if a bidder enters $14.05, your proxy bid will be $14.55. This happens instantly, so if you've ever been in a situation where you're being instantaneously outbid—this is the power of proxy bidding! Only when a bid higher than your $15.00 maximum is entered by another bidder will your proxy bids be exhausted. You will then be sent an email by eBay alerting you to the fact that you have been outbid and asking whether you would like to increase your proxy bid amount.

Some eBay sites allow sellers to set a reserve price for their auctions. This means there is an undisclosed minimum amount the seller requires before the product will be sold. If you're bidding on auctions on international eBay sites, you may receive a notification that the reserve price is not met. You can either increase your maximum bid amount to try to meet the reserve or let the auction run its course to see whether other bids increase the amount naturally.

Another form of bidding is known as sniping. Neither condoned nor outlawed by eBay, sniping utilises software that is capable of outbidding opponents in the dying seconds (sometimes milliseconds) of an auction. eBay does not provide sniping functionality, but you can find and download your own sniping software by conducting an internet search.

Once you have entered your chosen bid amount, click *Place bid*. A pop-up will appear asking you to confirm your bid (see figure 6.2). Review the information carefully (including any postage costs that are additional to your bid amount), and either click *Confirm bid* to commit to paying your entered amount should you be the highest bidder, or <u>Change bid</u> if you wish to enter a different bid amount. Once you hit *Confirm bid*, eBay will instantly display whether you are the current highest bidder or whether another bidder has outbid you.

Figure 6.2: confirming your bid

If you're the highest bidder, it's now just a waiting game. You need to wait until the auction end time (displayed at the top of the View item page and also on search results pages) to see whether your bid is high enough to fend off all other bidders. If you are outbid during the course of the auction, eBay will send you an email to alert you and ask whether you would like to increase your bid amount to stay in the auction. If you're the highest bidder at the close of the auction, you'll get a notification from eBay to congratulate you on your win with instructions for payment, and possibly also an email from your seller advising payment instructions. We'll cover paying for items in chapter 7.

In certain circumstances, you can retract your bid amount after you have hit the *Confirm bid* button. It is generally advised against, but there may be some honest situations where you've genuinely made a mistake. You can retract a bid only in the following circumstances:

- you made an error when entering your bid, such as bidding $50 instead of $5

- the item's description changed significantly after you placed your bid

- you haven't been able to reach the seller (emails bounce back or calls don't go through).

You need to be aware that there are rules around when a bid may be retracted. You must act before the final 12 hours of the auction (in this case all of your bids during the auction are retracted) or, if within the last 12 hours, you must retract the bid within one hour of making it (in this case only your most recent bid is retracted). You can also ask your seller for special permission to retract your bid during the last 12 hours of the auction. To retract a bid, click Customer support at top right of any eBay screen then enter 'bid retraction' in eBay's Help search box.

If you win, you pay!

Remember, if you're the winning bidder of an auction you are contractually bound to complete the sale by paying for the item.

For iPad and iPhone, from the View item page click the *Place bid* button. Enter your maximum bid amount, then, for iPhone, click the *Review* button, review your bid details then click the *Place bid* button; for iPad, click the *Place bid* button, review your bid details then click the *Confirm bid* button (see figure 6.3).

Figure 6.3: the iPad Confirm bid screen

To increase your bid amount at any time, go back to the View item page and click the *Increase max bid* button at the top; on your eBay app screen click the *Increase Bid* button. You can also do this from within the Buy/Buying section of My eBay by clicking on <u>Increase max bid</u>.

Items you bid on will be automatically added to your cart, but you will not be able to proceed to checkout unless you are the winner of the auction.

Buy an item listed as Buy it now

The steps for buying an item listed in the Buy it now format are quite similar to those used at auction. From the View item page you have the option to click the *Buy it now* or *Add to cart* buttons (see figure 6.4). *Add to cart* will automatically place the item in your shopping cart for you to check out at a later stage, perhaps after you've added more items that you're interested in purchasing. Note that the item is not reserved for you if you add it to your cart; it's yours only after you have paid for it! You can access your cart at any time by clicking the <u>Cart</u> link at top right of any eBay screen.

Figure 6.4: Buy it now or add to cart from the View item page

Alternatively, click the *Buy it now* button to pay for the item immediately. On the next page of checkout, review the item's details and price then click *Commit to buy* (see figure 6.5). On the next screen, click the blue *Pay now* button. We'll cover paying for items in the next chapter.

Figure 6.5: commit to buy

Some sellers utilise a feature known as Immediate payment required. This means that even if you commit to buy the item it will not be yours until the seller has received payment, or, to put another way, until you actually pay for the item the product remains available to other buyers.

The auction with Buy it now format

Some sellers choose to list their items in a combination of the auction and the Buy it now formats. In this instance, you will see three button options: *Place bid*, *Buy it now* and *Add to cart* (see figure 6.6). This means you have a choice of how you purchase the item: you can take your chances by bidding against others in the hope that you can get a great deal, or you can buy the item at the set Buy it now price specified by the seller. Once any bids have been made, the Buy it now price disappears and the listing automatically reverts to the standard rules of auction; the normal process for Buy it now or *Add to cart* is followed if you choose either of those options (as discussed earlier in this chapter). Note that if you click the *Add to cart* button and do not pay for the item, both auction and Buy it now options will remain available to other bidders/buyers until the seller has received your payment.

Figure 6.6: auction with Buy it now format

Each eBay site has different rules for the disparity between the auction start price and the Buy it now price. eBay Australia's policy is that the auction start price and Buy it now price can be the same (although this policy is also under review). For UK sellers, on the other hand, the Buy it now price must be 40 per cent higher.

Make an offer

Another way sellers can choose to sell an item is via the Buy it now format but with the option of having buyers make counter-offers. In other words, the seller sets a price of, say, $10 and allows buyers to make offers less than that amount. Sellers can choose to automatically reject offers below a certain minimum or to review all offers manually. In this case, three buttons will appear: *Buy it now*, *Add to cart* and *Make offer* (see figure 6.7).

Figure 6.7: making an offer

To make an offer, click the **Make offer** button. On the pop-up that appears, make your best offer, specify the quantity of the items you would like (often ordering higher quantities will encourage sellers to accept your lower price), click **Review offer**, then on the final screen click **Submit offer**.

For iPad and iPhone, click the **Make offer** button, then on the next screen enter your offer amount plus any contractual terms for the seller to consider. Next click the **Review** button on the iPhone, or the **Review offer** button on the iPad (see figure 6.8).

Figure 6.8: making on offer on iPad

If the seller has used an automatic review system, your offer will be accepted or rejected instantly; otherwise eBay will notify you of your seller's decision within 48 hours via email.

Second chance offers

From time to time you may also receive what is known as a second chance offer from a seller after a listing ends. A second chance offer can occur when the original buyer of the product can no longer fulfil their payment obligations, the auction's reserve price was not met, or perhaps the seller has two of the same item to sell and would like to offer you the chance to buy one of them. You're under no obligation to accept the offer from the seller and you should always ensure the offer is genuine before proceeding.

Verifying second chance offers

There are three ways to ensure a second chance offer is genuine:

*   On the View item page you'll see the following message: 'You have received a second chance offer for this item.' To view the details and purchase the item, click the Second chance offer link.

*   In Messages within My eBay you'll see a Second Chance Offer email from eBay in your inbox.

*   In My eBay go to the *Activity* tab. Under the 'Buy' heading, click Didn't win.

Classified ads

Some categories on eBay also include the classifieds format. In essence, a classified ad does not involve transacting online and is like a traditional 'for sale' notice you might see on your local community noticeboard. The seller gives you information regarding what is for sale and for what price, and if you're interested in buying it you contact the seller to arrange for payment and pick-up. When shopping for cars on eBay, you may come across a classified ad with Best offer. If you make an offer on the car and it is accepted by the seller, you have committed to paying for your purchase. Best offers can be paid for via eBay's checkout, depending on the payment methods the seller chooses to accept.

Chapter 7
Paying for an item

Now that we've won an auction, committed to buying the item or added it to our cart, it's time to pay for it. On eBay there are four main ways of paying for an item during checkout. We'll cover each of these in detail and outline other payment options.

Pay with PayPal

PayPal, which is an eBay company, is the most popular way to pay for products purchased on eBay. The vast majority of sellers accept it for all of their products and some sellers specify it as their preferred payment option. PayPal is also one of the safest methods of paying for anything online, because you never share any of your personal or financial information; the only information buyers and sellers exchange is their email address. PayPal keeps all members' financial information safely encrypted, and using PayPal you can pay for your items via credit card, a bank account, a positive PayPal balance (achieved by receiving funds into your PayPal account if you sell products online, or by transferring funds into PayPal from your bank account) or a PayPal gift voucher (as awarded by eBay, PayPal or another online business). This method also means you don't have to enter your credit card or other financial details every time you pay for an item; you just log into your PayPal account using your email address and password.

It costs you nothing to pay for online purchases using PayPal unless you purchase an item in a foreign currency, in which case a currency conversion fee is charged. The conversion is made at PayPal's wholesale exchange rate, to which is added a percentage fee of between 2.5 and 4 per cent, depending on the currency and whether the conversion is made as part of a purchase or is a straight transfer of funds.

Another feature of using PayPal is that you may be covered for purchases of up to $20 000, providing real peace of mind whenever you spend money online. We'll cover PayPal Buyer protection in chapter 8.

Let's take a moment to register for a PayPal account now—this will mean you are ready to pay for items as soon as you've confirmed your registration.

Registering for a PayPal account

☐ Go to the PayPal homepage at www.paypal.com.au and click on the *Sign up* button at top right, or the *Sign up now* button on the left (see figure 7.1).

☐ On the next page, there are three types of PayPal accounts to choose from: Personal, Premier and Business. Choose the account that is right for you (opt for Personal if you intend only to buy online, Premier if you intend to buy and sell, and Business if you want to sell a lot). Click the *Get started* button for the type of account you want. In this example, we chose Personal.

☐ On the next page, fill in all of your personal information. Remember, you need do this only once.

☐ Choose to link your credit card (or a debit card with the Visa or MasterCard logo) so you can start shopping right away. Currently only Visa and MasterCard credit cards are accepted by PayPal. Not linking your credit card will mean your PayPal account will take a few days to become active, and paying via the bank can be delayed for up to five days (more on this later in the chapter). Also, linking your credit card means you can earn frequent flyer points whenever you fund a PayPal transaction via a credit card linked to a frequent flyer program.

☐ Click the *Agree and create account* button.

☐ On the next page, enter the security code then click *Continue*. That's it! You now have an active PayPal account.

☐ It's a good idea to link your bank account straightaway, as this gives you added flexibility in choosing how to pay for goods bought online. Click Link your bank account, or from the PayPal homepage click My account then Profile then Add or edit bank account.

☐ On the next page, enter your bank details then click *Continue*. Review your bank account information carefully then click *Save*. PayPal will deposit two small amounts into your nominated account to verify your identity (you get to keep these funds). Once received, log back into PayPal to verify the amounts by clicking My account then Overview and either Get verified or Complete bank setup.

Figure 7.1: the PayPal Australia homepage

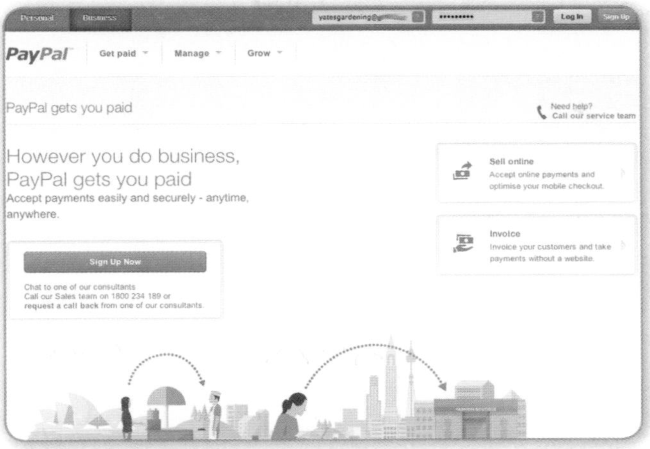

Choosing a password

Make your PayPal password different from your eBay password, and never share it with anyone. It's a good idea to change your password every few months and to use a combination of letters and numbers that's easy for you to remember but difficult for anyone else to guess. Do not use any component of your email address, as this could be easy for people to guess.

If you'd like to add funds to your PayPal account so you can pay for products instantly without worrying about credit card charges or bank processing delays, once you've linked your bank account click <u>My account</u> then <u>Add funds</u> then <u>Transfer funds from a bank account in Australia</u>. It will take three to five business days for the funds to appear in your PayPal account.

Now we have a registered PayPal account, let's pay for an eBay item using PayPal. In chapter 6 we progressed from the View item page right through the auction bidding process and up to committing to buy an item or adding it to our cart. Once you've clicked on *Commit to buy*, or in your cart clicked *Proceed to checkout*, or from your winning bidder email notification clicked on *Pay now*, you're ready to pay for your product(s). Here is an illustrated example of the steps involved.

First click *Commit to buy* (see figure 7.2). Review your order details carefully and check the PayPal box as your chosen payment method. Click *Continue*.

Figure 7.2: commit to buy

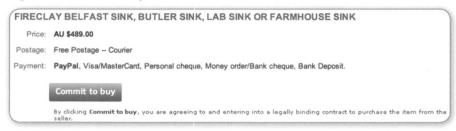

Next log into PayPal using your email address and PayPal password. Choose your payment funding source (for example, PayPal balance, credit card or bank). The default will be PayPal balance if you have a positive balance, although you can change this by clicking Change (see figure 7.3). Note also in figure 7.3 that if you have a PayPal voucher you can access these funds by clicking Redeem; you'll then be asked to enter the voucher's code.

Figure 7.3: choose your PayPal funding source

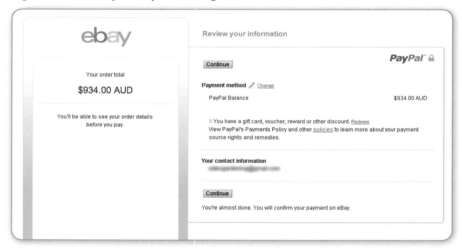

On the next page click *Confirm and pay* (see figure 7.4). You'll then see a notification confirming, and thanking you for, your payment. The amount will be debited from your chosen funding source and your seller will be notified that you have paid for your item.

Figure 7.4: confirm your order and pay

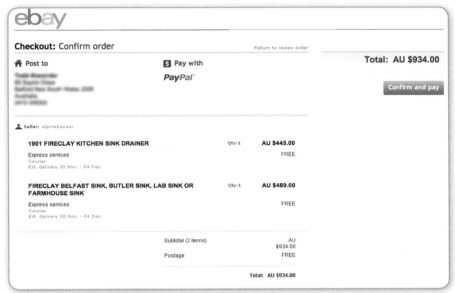

 For iPad and iPhone, after clicking *Commit to buy* click *Pay now*. If you're already logged into PayPal on your iPad, it will verify your account; if not, it will ask you to sign in to PayPal. On the confirm order screen (see figure 7.5, overleaf), confirm your order and choose your PayPal funding source. Click *Confirm & pay*. That's it, you're done!

Figure 7.5: paying with PayPal via the eBay app

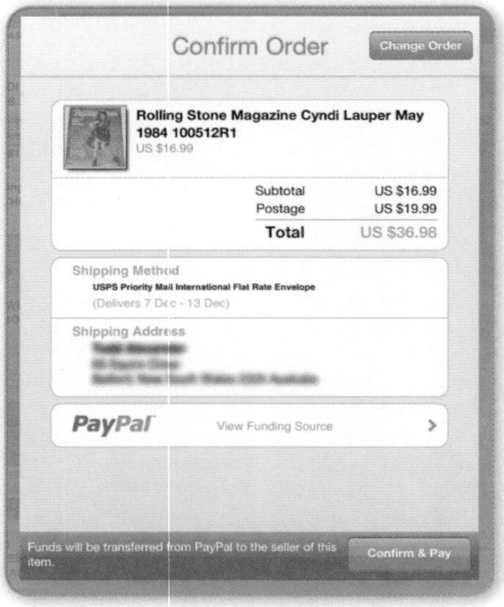

If you don't have a credit card or Visa/MasterCard debit card linked to your PayPal account, a payment funded by your linked bank account is known as an eCheque. These are not instant fund transfers and will take anywhere from three to five working days to appear in your seller's PayPal account, depending on your bank's processing times. To ensure you receive your items as quickly as possible, link a credit or debit card to your PayPal account and ensure you have verified your bank account as outlined previously in this chapter. You will still be able to pay via bank transfer, but the transaction will happen instantly because you have a back-up funding source should you not have enough money in your bank account to cover it.

You can also access PayPal via its mobile apps. Check with your smartphone or tablet app store for the latest release PayPal mobile products.

Pay with credit card

Some eBay sellers have merchant credit card processing capabilities and accept payment by credit card. Paying for a purchase using a credit card is not incorporated into the eBay checkout process. To pay by credit card, where the option is available, check the 'Merchant account—credit card' box then click *Continue* (see figure 7.6). The seller will be notified that you have completed checkout and will get in touch with you to arrange payment via credit card, usually by taking your credit card details over the telephone.

Figure 7.6: paying with credit card, cheque or bank deposit

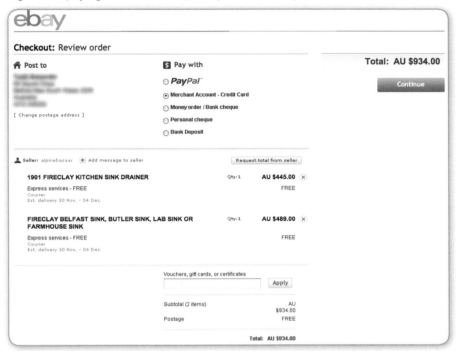

Tips on purchasing by credit card

While PayPal offers Buyer protection, most financial institutions also have a facility called credit card chargeback that can be utilised in the event that you do not receive the goods you have purchased, or if the goods are faulty or significantly different from the seller's description. Check with your provider so you know your rights when purchasing via credit card. It's also a good idea to keep a small limit on a credit card you use frequently to purchase products online, as if anything does go wrong and your details fall into a criminal's hands, you've automatically limited your potential for loss. Always check your credit card transaction history very carefully and notify your provider immediately if you see something strange on your statement.

Paying for an item

Pay via bank deposit

One reason some eBay sellers choose to accept bank transfers is because it costs them nothing to accept your payment (PayPal and credit card providers charge sellers a small percentage fee per transaction). Where the option is available, to pay via bank transfer check the 'Bank deposit' box during checkout then click *Continue* (see figure 7.6, p. 65). Sellers who accept bank transfers will usually share their bank details with you during the checkout process; if they do not, contact them and ask for the information. You will then have to log into your financial institution's online banking site or go into a local branch of the seller's bank to arrange to have the funds transferred. When completing your transfer online, it's always a good idea to include your eBay user ID as a reference for the payment so the seller can quickly identify the payment as yours.

Bank transfers can take between three and five days to be processed, so be patient if you're using this method and send your seller an email to let them know you've paid. You should be aware that most financial institutions are unable to reverse a bank transfer, so it's very important you check the details carefully, because in the event that something goes wrong you may have no recourse from your financial provider.

Pay with Paymate

Paymate is an Australian company that offers a service very similar to PayPal. It is one of the accepted payment methods on eBay, though its adoption by sellers is still relatively low. Unlike PayPal, Paymate does not store your financial information so you do not need to sign up to become a Paymate member. If your seller does accept Paymate, choose that option during checkout and enter your credit card details securely via Paymate, which will notify the seller that you have paid — no financial information is shared. For more information on Paymate, head to the website at www.paymate.com.au. It no longer costs buyers an additional fee to pay using Paymate.

Other payment methods

Although this is less common on eBay, some sellers will also allow other forms of payment.

Cash

Never send cash in the mail! If it gets lost there is no way you can replace it. If your seller accepts cash on pick-up, after you have carefully inspected the goods, pay cash in person. It's a good idea to ask the seller to sign an invoice (take one with you) or other written confirmation that you have paid cash and taken the goods with you. Be careful carrying large sums of cash and make sure you take someone with you for added security. There is no buyer protection scheme for payments made with cash.

Money orders and cheques

Some eBay sellers will allow you to pay for items by sending a cheque or money order. It can take up to seven working days for cheques to clear so there may be some delay before you receive your goods from the seller.

Avoid Western Union and MoneyGram

eBay does not allow the use of internet money transfers such as Western Union and MoneyGram, as tracking these payments can be impossible. In addition, they come with no buyer protection. Never ask your seller to let you pay using one of these methods; if the seller asks for one of them, do not agree, and alert eBay immediately.

Success!

Once you have completed checkout successfully and paid for your product(s), you'll receive a success notification from eBay (see figure 7.7) and an email for your records. On the success notification there are links to <u>View your order details</u>, to track your order by clicking <u>Go to my eBay</u> and, on the right, to share your purchase with friends via *email*, *Facebook* and *Twitter*.

Figure 7.7: successful checkout notification

Chapter 8
Keeping track of purchases in My eBay

My eBay is like your own eBay diary. It keeps track of all your buying activity so you can return to it any time to complete certain actions. Some of us get so carried away bidding on, and buying, products that we lose track of just what we're purchasing. My eBay keeps a record of everything for you. To access My eBay, click on the link at top right of any eBay page. You can also hover your mouse over this link to choose to go to a specific section within My eBay. Let's go through each of the areas of My eBay together.

Whenever you click on My eBay, the navigation area will appear on the left (see figure 8.1). In this chapter we'll cover the buying-related sections of My eBay.

Figure 8.1: My eBay navigation

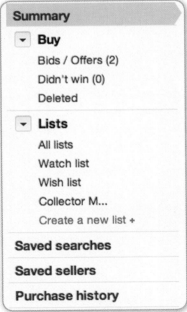

iPhone For iPhone, access by clicking *My eBay* at the bottom of your home screen. Watched items can be accessed by clicking the *Watching* button on your home screen. To access saved searches and sellers, click the Saved link on the home screen (see figure 1.2, p. 4).

iPad For iPad, watched items can be accessed by clicking the blue *Watching* button on the home screen and saved searches will automatically appear on your home screen (a star in an orange bubble will mark a saved search). Click the *Buying* button on the home screen for other My eBay functionality. One of the cool features of the iPad app is that you can simply flick through your watched or buying lists by sliding your fingers across the images that appear. You can also access My eBay by clicking the green navigation tab at top left of any screen (see figure 1.3, p. 5).

The Summary page

The Summary page gives an overview of all of your currently active buying activity, including watch lists, bids and offers. Let's take a look at the various functionalities on the page (see figure 8.2).

Above the watch list grey bar is a link for Page options. Clicking on this lets you specify what you would like to see on your summary page. (For example, you can choose to add purchases, saved searches, lists and selling activity). Next to this it tells you what the default My eBay landing page is. Click Change to alter your landing page.

Towards the right end of the grey bar will be a link for Edit and a drop-down arrow. You can change the colours on the page, and by clicking on Customise in the pop-up that appears you can change the information that appears in each section. Click the up or down arrow to the right of each section to move it up or down the page.

Beneath the watch list bar are three links: All, Active and Ended. Click on these to view the corresponding listings. The number of listings in each category is shown in brackets after the link. On the right you can change the sort order of the list by clicking the drop-down arrow next to 'Sort by'. You can choose to sort by time, price, date or seller. Click on one of the column headers (Bids, Price and so on) to sort the list by that criteria (lowest to highest, or highest to lowest).

The listing information appears next: product image, item title, seller name, feedback score, feedback rating and quantity available. You can click on most of these to view the corresponding listing or feedback information. Over to the right is the corresponding information for each column (Bids, Price and so on).

The far right column is for Actions. There are three links: Buy it now begins the checkout process. Get IM alerts can send you instant messages when the listing is about to end or you have been outbid. By clicking on More actions you can contact the seller, View seller's store, View seller's other items, View similar items from other sellers, Save the seller to your favourite sellers list, Add a note for your own reference or Add to list (add the listing to a list for future reference).

Note the check box next to the product image. You can click this (and multiple listings) to add a note, delete, compare products or add to list. The grey buttons for these functions appear beneath all items on your watch list.

Figure 8.2: My eBay summary

Buy

The Buy section of My eBay works in exactly the same way as the Summary section, outlined previously, except the lists are of products you have bid on or made an offer on (Bids/Offers), products you did not win (at auction or where your offers were rejected by the seller — Didn't win), and listings you have previously deleted from one of your lists (Deleted).

Lists

As covered in chapter 5, you can click one of three options from the View item page: Add to watch list, or use the drop-down arrow next to this to access Add to wish list and Add to a new list (see figure 5.1, p. 41). Any product added to one of these lists will automatically be collated in the Lists section of My eBay. You can create a new list at any time by clicking Add to a new list and creating a title for that list (note in figure 8.1, on p. 69, we have created a list called 'Collector Movies'). You can share new lists and wish lists with your family and friends via email and Facebook. You might want to send your kids' birthday wish list to their grandparents, for example.

For iPhone, you can only create a watch list (click *Watch* at top right of the View item screen). If you'd like to share a listing with friends, you must do so one at a time rather than via a wish list or new list. To do so, click *Share this item* at the bottom of the View item screen (see figure 5.5, p. 48).

For iPad, only watch and share functionalities apply. To watch, click the *eye icon* next to the word *Watch* at the top of the View item screen; to share, click the *arrow icon* next to the word Share (see figure 5.6, p. 49).

Saved searches/sellers

As covered in chapter 2, when you create a search you love, you can save this search to My eBay and return to it anytime you like, rather than having to try to recreate it each time. All saved searches or sellers you have added to your saved seller list will appear in these areas of My eBay.

Purchase history

Any item that you've completed payment for will appear in the Purchase history section of My eBay (see figure 8.3). Let's take a closer look at the functionality on this page.

Check the relevant box at the top of the page to see Recent or Archived purchases (older than 60 days). Choose one of the links to see All products, those Awaiting payment, Posted or Awaiting feedback. Beneath this, change the period from 'Last 60 days' to 'Last 31 days', 'Current week' or 'Current month'. On the right, next to 'Sort by', change for the most recently bought item or the item bought the longest time ago.

The listing information is the same as for the watch list outlined earlier in this chapter. Note on this page that if the seller has uploaded a tracking number, you will be able to track the progress of the product's delivery. Estimated delivery also appears when the time frame to receive the product is longer than expected.

On the right, after 'Price' you will see four grey icons: a dollar sign, an envelope, a star next to a pencil, and a star. Each of these icons represents an activity completed by either seller or buyer, and each changes from grey to blue once completed. The dollar sign means you have paid for the product; the envelope means the seller has marked the product as shipped; the pencil means you have left feedback for the transaction; and the star means you have received feedback from the seller.

Finally, to the far right are three links: <u>Leave feedback</u>, <u>Contact seller</u> / <u>Track package</u>, and <u>More actions</u>. As covered in chapter 1, <u>Leave feedback</u> for the seller once you have received your product and are happy with it. You can <u>Contact the seller</u> to ask any question regarding your transaction by clicking the link; <u>Track package</u> will appear if the seller has uploaded a shipping tracking number, and clicking on this will show a pop-up of where your parcel is. <u>More actions</u> include: view order details, sell this item, contact seller, return this item, resolve a problem, view PayPal transaction, unmark as payment sent, view seller's other items, view similar items, save this seller and add note.

You can archive older items (with no outstanding actions) by checking the box next to the product image, scrolling down the page and clicking the *Archive* button.

Figure 8.3: Purchase history in My eBay

My Messages

In figure 8.2, p. 71, note the *Messages* tab at the top of the screen. Also known as My Messages, this is where all communication from your sellers and eBay will appear. It's important always to check that messages appear here, as only messages from genuine sellers (and eBay or PayPal) appear in the Messages section of My eBay. Here you can respond to communications from sellers, save communications between you and the seller, and keep track of important changes to eBay and other information from the company.

Chapter 9
Troubleshooting purchases

If you've done your research thoroughly, taken the time to read the item description carefully and reviewed your seller's trading reputation, it's very unlikely that anything will go wrong with your purchase. However, from time to time you may find the need to troubleshoot. Your package may not have arrived in the mail, for example, or the item may be broken or not as described by the seller. In this chapter we'll explore all the options available to you to ensure your experience while using eBay is enjoyable and safe.

First contact the seller

Always contact your seller *before* taking any action such as leaving negative feedback or lodging a complaint with eBay or PayPal. The vast majority of eBay sellers will be only too happy to provide you with a satisfactory solution, whether an exchange or replacement product, or a partial or total refund. Only if the seller does not respond, or does not respond satisfactorily, should you take further action.

I changed my mind

Sometimes we might experience buyer's remorse and decide we no longer want to proceed with a purchase. Up until the point that your seller dispatches the product, it is possible to contact them and ask to cancel the transaction. Some sellers will be happy to do so, though you should use this sparingly as it adds administration and work for the seller, and it could mean the product is never sold again. If you do wish to cancel your transaction, contact the seller as soon as possible and ask politely. This can be done, at the seller's discretion, before or after you have paid for the product, so long as it has not left the seller's possession. Note that refunds via PayPal, Paymate, bank or credit card are much easier to arrange than if you have paid by cash, cheque or money order.

I have not received my item

The first thing to do is go back to the View item page and read the description thoroughly to ensure you are aware of the expected window of delivery. You can also find this information in the Purchase history section of My eBay, or perhaps the seller has emailed you via Messages to let you know of a possible delay. If you're unable to find the information, or if the date has passed, contact the seller to ask for an update on delivery status. Where the seller has uploaded a tracking number, always check this first and if anything is unclear or out of the ordinary, ask the seller to explain.

If you have a deadline for delivery (for example, you're buying a present for someone's birthday), it's a good idea to contact the seller *before* purchasing the item to confirm that your deadline will be met.

If the seller insists they have sent the item and you still have not received it after a reasonable amount of time, you can either follow up with the seller again, contact your local post or courier distributor, or access eBay's resolution centre (covered later in this chapter).

The product is broken / faulty / not as described

Good eBay sellers take extra care when packaging items to ensure they will not be damaged in transit, but breakages can still sometimes occur. Perhaps you receive an orange product rather than the red one you requested, one brand instead of another, glass instead of crystal. Re-read the item description to check the condition and all other details of the item.

You might receive the product in good condition but find there is a fault with the way it operates. This may be a manufacturer fault that the seller is not even aware of. Some products sold on eBay come with the manufacturer's warranty, and you may need to return the product to the manufacturer rather than to the eBay seller, as is standard for some products sold by retailers.

In each of these circumstances, contact the seller to explain the problem and ask for a refund or a replacement product. Some sellers will ask you to return the faulty product to them. Check the seller's returns policy within the item description, because you may be required to pay for return postage (just as you would be responsible for physically returning a product to a retail store). If the seller does not offer a satisfactory solution, contact eBay's resolution centre.

The product is not right for me

An article of clothing may not fit well, an electrical part may not match the device you're trying to fix or a DVD may not be coded to play in your region. It's your responsibility to ensure you've read the item description thoroughly, and if the seller has clearly specified the information you may not qualify for a refund or replacement. If you're worried about clothing sizes, check the seller's returns policy before purchasing—some are happy to exchange sizes, no questions asked. In this case, you would be able to lodge a claim for this transaction only if the product was not as the seller described it.

eBay's resolution centre

If the seller cannot resolve your situation, you can lodge a claim with eBay via its resolution centre. The easiest way to do this is to go to your purchase history in My eBay (as covered in chapter 8) and click More actions (to the right of the product details) then Resolve a problem. In the resolution centre, notify eBay of the problem you're having and they will work with you and the seller to discuss, track and resolve your case. If you've paid using PayPal, you'll automatically be directed to the PayPal resolution centre as PayPal's buyer protection may cover you.

(iPhone) To access the resolution centre via iPhone, click *Settings* at the bottom of your home screen then *Contact eBay support* then Buying, then click one of the links under eBay Buyer Protection: Didn't receive an item or Item wasn't as described.

(iPad) For iPad, from the navigation area on the left click Settings then contact eBay support.

Troubleshooting purchases

PayPal buyer protection

Under PayPal's buyer protection scheme, your purchase may be covered for up to $20 000, including price paid and original shipping costs. Buyer protection operates when you have not received an item or the item is significantly different from how the seller described it. The following situations may be covered by buyer protection:

- You purchased your item on eBay (that is, you used eBay's checkout process to pay for the goods).
- You used PayPal to pay for the item.
- You used the seller's email address associated with the listing.
- The sale was for a physical item.
- You filed only one claim per PayPal payment.
- You opened the case within 45 days of payment and escalated it to a claim (if needed) within 20 days of opening the case.
- You and the eBay listing meet the buyer protection guidelines as outlined on the PayPal website.

For direct access, click Resolution centre under My account at the PayPal website. The seller has seven days to respond to your claim and if they have not done so, or have not provided a resolution within 20 days, you can escalate your complaint to a claim for retrieval of your PayPal funds. PayPal will notify you of the outcome of the claim and, if awarded, the refund will appear as a credit in your PayPal account.

You can track the progress of your claims within the PayPal resolution centre, the eBay resolution centre or your purchase history within My eBay. If you have any problems accessing the resolution centre, tracking your claim or contacting your seller, contact eBay's customer support team as outlined in chapter 1.

Other resolutions

As covered in chapter 7, some financial institutions allow you to challenge a credit card payment if you do not receive an internet purchase paid for by credit card, or if the product was significantly different from how the seller described it. It can take anywhere from seven to 40 days for your bank to process a claim.

Paymate offers buyer protection for any purchase made from a Paymate TrustMark seller (more information can be found on its website). Click Resources at the top of the homepage then click Buyer protection program.

Buying TOP 10

10 things you need to know about buying products on eBay

1   Always read the item description thoroughly so you know exactly what you're purchasing, as well as all the information about your seller and their terms of trade.

2   Use a combination of advanced search and eBay's search filters to narrow down your results to products that best suit your needs. Save your favourite searches and sellers so you can keep returning to them without having to enter the information again.

3   Not sure of something? Ask eBay's customer support team for help. You can call them on the phone, email them or use live chat—they'll even call you.

4   eBay's Deals offer hundreds of products from some of eBay's best sellers at heavily discounted prices, often with free shipping.

5   Use share features to tell your friends and family about the things you love on eBay, or create a wish list for special occasions.

6   If something does go wrong with the transaction, always contact your seller before taking further action. Most sellers will exchange or replace an item or offer you a refund.

7   Paying with PayPal can mean you're covered for up to $20 000 on qualifying purchases.

8   Refer to the bargain-hunting tips in chapter 2 to get ahead of other buyers and score some amazing deals.

9   Track all of your buying activity through My eBay—from here you can complete most tasks associated with buying.

10 Leave positive feedback for your sellers when you're happy with your experience. Feedback helps make eBay a better marketplace for everyone.

PART III

Selling a product (Basic selling)

Questions answered in this part

(continued)

Questions answered in this part *(cont'd)*

Chapter 13: Keeping track of listings using My eBay
- What is My eBay?
- How do I answer questions from buyers?
- How do I relist an unsold item?

Chapter 14: Accepting payments
- What is PayPal and how do I accept PayPal payments?
- Can I receive payment directly into my bank account?
- Are there other forms of payment I can receive from buyers?

Chapter 15: Postage and handling tips
- Should I offer free postage?
- What types of postage can I use?
- How do I package my products properly?

Chapter 16: Customer service
- How do I provide great customer service?
- When should I leave feedback for buyers?

Chapter 17: eBay's selling fees
- How much does it cost to sell on eBay?
- How much does it cost to accept PayPal payments?
- What are optional listing upgrades?

Chapter 18: Troubleshooting for eBay sellers
- What if my buyer doesn't pay?
- What if my item doesn't sell?
- What if a buyer complains about me?

Chapter 10
An introduction to selling

While most eBay members use the site to buy great new products, eBay remains Australia's most popular website for selling second-hand goods. Millions of Australians have used eBay as a way to supplement their income, or finance their purchases by making a few extra dollars selling things they no longer need. A few years ago, before I started my eBay business, I sold a lot of unwanted items from around my house. I've often shared the story that when I renovated my house I needed to get rid of about four skips' worth of unwanted clutter such as doors, windows, security grilles and even a kitchenette. I didn't think there was any value in these items and was prepared to pay the $1600 for the four skips needed to take all that stuff away for landfill. But as an eBay employee I thought I really should give selling it a go … and was amazed to find that after two weeks I'd sold it all for around $3500. Add the price of the skips I no longer needed and allow for a few hours' work listing 50 items on eBay, and the experience netted me $5100. And it didn't all end up in landfill.

Not everyone will have an un-renovated house to clear, but we all have possessions we no longer need, use or want. Turning these into cash is much easier than you might think.

When I ask people why they aren't selling on eBay, one of the most common replies is, 'I have nothing to sell'. Take a moment now to think about all the things in your home you no longer use—DVDs you never watch, clothes you haven't worn for more than a year, that piece of furniture sitting in the garage, the exercise equipment you bought with the best of intentions … the list goes on. For inspiration on what you can sell, visit the eBay what to sell page—hover your mouse over <u>Sell</u> at the top of any eBay page and click <u>What to sell</u>. Click on any of the highlighted household items to see a completed items search with prices achieved.

eBay also has an introduction to selling page that includes helpful videos, step-by-step guides and frequently asked questions about selling. It's a great place to start your eBay selling and it's a handy reference point to come back to if you need a bit of help along the way. To visit the page, hover your mouse over Sell at the top of any eBay page and click How to sell.

Chapter 11

Registering as an eBay seller

While eBay will allow you to begin the selling process without a seller account, you will eventually need to register as a seller. This is an additional step in your eBay registration to the ones covered in chapter 1.

Link your PayPal account to eBay

One of the easiest ways to receive funds for the items you sell is to accept PayPal. In part II we completed PayPal registration. Later in part III we'll cover more on how to accept funds via PayPal. Linking your PayPal and eBay accounts is a simple once-only process.

To link accounts, click _My eBay_ at the top of any eBay page then click *Account* then _PayPal account_ (see figure 11.1). If you haven't already completed your PayPal registration, click *Sign up*; to link accounts click *Link My PayPal account*. Clicking *Sign up* will take you through the PayPal registration process as covered in part II. *Link my PayPal account* will take you to a screen where you need to enter your PayPal email address and your PayPal password then click *Link your account*. On the next screen, click *Return to eBay*. Once you've completed this process you'll automatically be able to receive funds into your PayPal account for the items you sell on eBay.

Figure 11.1: linking your eBay and PayPal accounts

Nominate a payment method for eBay fees

You'll also need to nominate how you would like to pay your eBay fees. You can either choose an automated payment option or make one-off payments when you have an outstanding amount to be paid. To choose your fee-payment method, click My eBay at the top of any eBay page then click *Account* then *Personal information* (see figure 11.2). Under the heading 'Financial information' click:

- Automatic payment method — to have your fees automatically debited from your PayPal account, debit card or credit card

- One-time payment — to make a once-only payment using PayPal, direct debit, credit card or cheque (click on the relevant link on the next page). Note you will only be able to do this if you have sold an item and incurred some eBay fees.

Figure 11.2: nominating a fee payment method

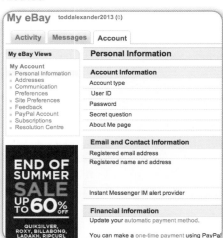

Verify your identity

If you have not linked your PayPal account or specified a fee-payment method, at some point in the selling process eBay will ask you to verify your identity. This is usually done by eBay sending you an automated phone call with a four-digit PIN (personal identification number) to enter on the eBay site. This is a simple process; just follow the prompts if you're asked to enter your PIN.

Chapter 12
Listing an item for sale

There are four different ways to list an item for sale on eBay. Two different forms can be used via the website, and you can also list items from your iPhone or iPad. In this chapter, we'll cover examples for listing on eBay Australia with an option to send your products to international destinations. Another option, though, is to go directly to a foreign eBay site and list directly. This will mean your product appears on that site in the local currency, which can be particularly beneficial if you have a product likely to be popular in another country. To list on a foreign site, the steps will be similar to those outlined in this chapter and you simply need to log onto the relevant site directly (a list of all eBay sites can be found at the bottom of the eBay homepage).

Before we begin, as every great listing requires a great product photograph, let's start by covering a few photo-taking tips to help with your selling success.

Take great photos of your products

Some eBay sites have recently made it mandatory to add a photo of the product you are selling. Listings without photographs tend not to attract buyers or, if they do, tend to be sold for very low prices. Always add the best quality image of what you're selling to give buyers a visual and very clear summary of what is for sale. You can add more than one photo to your listing for no additional charge, so choose multiple angles. If there are flaws to the product, take close-ups to set clear buyer expectations.

Most products you sell will require you to use a camera to capture the image, but for products such as books and DVDs you can scan the items using a scanner attached to your computer. Always upload your own image and do not steal the copyrighted material of others by simply copying and pasting from an internet image search.

Here are some top photo-taking tips to help you maximise your eBay sales.

Tips on product photos

- Use natural lighting rather than a flash.

- Use a plain (preferably white) background.

- Avoid using zoom—move the camera closer to the product instead.

- For clothing, borrow a mannequin or ask a friend or family member to model. Try to position them in the most visually compelling way.

- Keep your image size large and upload the maximum size that eBay allows (for best quality use images of more than 1600 pixels in height or width).

- Never use software to overlay text on your image—buyers prefer a clean image.

- Think like a retailer: is your photo worthy of a place in the latest catalogue?

- Beware of reflections off shiny objects (we don't want to see you in your pyjamas!).

Complete the standard Sell your item form, step by step

Though it has changed in minor ways over time, the standard Sell your item form is essentially the same that eBay has provided for many years. You access the form by clicking Sell at the top of any eBay page. Remember you also have the option of using the Simple selling form, which is covered later in this chapter.

Let's complete a listing together using the example of a packet of tomato seeds.

Step 1: search for category

The first step is to find the most relevant category for your item. You can do this by entering a few product keywords about the item you want to list (in this example we entered 'tomato seeds') and click *Search* (see figure 12.1).

Note that for some products you can enter a product code. You can also click on the <u>Browse categories</u> link to choose from eBay's list of categories, or if you have listed before try <u>Recently used categories</u> (you will also see a link for <u>Select a product from your inventory</u> — we'll cover this in part IV of the book).

Figure 12.1: step 1 of the Sell your item form

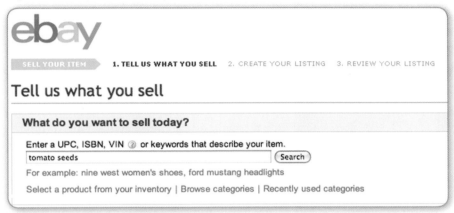

Step 2: choose category

In Step 2 choose the most relevant category for your item — categories are listed in order of relevance (in the example in figure 12.2 we chose 'Seeds & Bulbs'). Check the box then click *Continue*.

Figure 12.2: step 2 of the Sell your item form

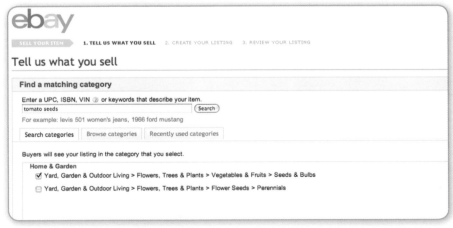

Choose the most logical category

Choosing the most relevant category for your item can impact where your listing appears on the search results page. Always choose the most logical category for your product (list accessories in an accessories category, not the device category, for example). If you're in doubt, search for your item on eBay and see what category most other sellers have listed it in. Where possible, avoid listing in categories named 'Other' as buyers tend not to browse through these less relevant categories.

Step 3: enter item specifics

In step 3 you include all the relevant information about your product. Remember to be as comprehensive as possible and to fill in all areas of the form. Think like a retailer describing their product for the latest catalogue, and try to leave no unanswered questions in your buyers' minds (see figure 12.3).

Figure 12.3: step 3 of the Sell your item form

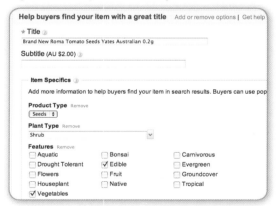

First create a compelling listing title. This should include all the most relevant keywords relating to the product. Include details specific to your item and category, such as colour, size, style, brand, weight, country of manufacture, year of manufacture, condition, material or gender. Don't use words that are only loosely associated with your product, as this may reduce the relevancy of your listing and limit its exposure on the site. In this example we have chosen 'Brand New Roma Tomato Seeds Yates Australian 0.2g'. Extraneous words would have been *plant*, *gardening* and *full sun*; by using these terms our listing would surface every time they were entered in a search by buyers, but because our product is only loosely associated with these terms, buyers would be unlikely to click on our listing, which would demote our overall relevance score under Best match (for more on Best match, see part IV).

Including a subtitle is optional and costs an additional fee. Subtitles can be viewed on search results pages and are helpful if you have a surplus of product keywords or want to convey important purchase information, such as free shipping or 100-day returns. In this example we have not entered a subtitle.

Describe the condition of your item. In some categories you will be able to choose from definitions provided by eBay; in others, such as this example, you will need to describe the condition of the item in your own words. We chose 'Brand new, Original manufacturer packaging, Never opened'.

Don't hide flaws

Don't be hesitant to outline all flaws of the product you are selling in great detail. The best tactic is to write a comprehensive bullet list and take a close-up photograph of each of the flaws. Particularly for used items, it is most important to set clear buyer expectations so potential customers know exactly what condition the product is in. While flawed products will naturally results in lower prices, not clearly labelling flaws will only lead to buyer disappointment and may lead to you receiving negative feedback, low ratings or the subject of a buyer dispute.

Listing an item for sale

Next describe your item specifics. The options for types of item specifics will change depending on what category you have listed your item in. Where possible, always specify aspects in the fields automatically provided by eBay. This part of the listing form is very important because providing this information can help with the exposure of your product, as it covers many of the search refinements buyers use. For this example, we clicked the Remove link next to the item specific for 'Model' then clicked Add your own item specific to enter 'Plant name: tomato'. You can add as many as you like but it's best to stick to the most important product features (similar to what you have chosen for your title).

Step 4: upload image

Scrolling down the page, next we add a photograph of the product (see figure 12.4). Note that some eBay sites will no longer allow you to list without a photo. First click *Add pictures* then in the pop-up that appears click *Browse*. Choose the image from where you've it saved on your computer then click *Open*. Your image will now appear in the pop-up.

Figure 12.4: step 4 of the Sell your item form

Use the *Crop*, *Rotate*, *Exposure* or *Brightness* functions on the right to improve the quality of your image (if necessary). Once complete, click *Upload* (see figure 12.5). You can add up to 12 photos for free on most eBay sites. (See earlier in this chapter for photo-taking tips.)

Figure 12.5: uploading the product photo

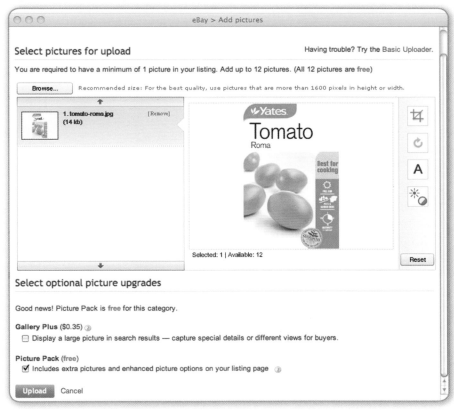

Step 5: describe the product

Next you need to describe the product as thoroughly as possible (see figure 12.6, overleaf). This information can be found on the packaging of the item, or you may have to do a little internet research to find out more about what you're selling. Be sure not to plagiarise by using other people's copyrighted information and images.

Figure 12.6: step 5 of the Sell your item form

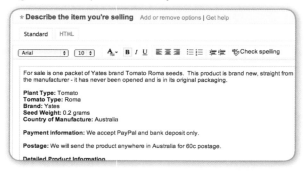

Note in our example that we have clearly set out the relevant product information in a list. It's also a good idea to include your payment, postage and returns policies within this area of the listing. Use the links at the top of the description builder to change font styles and colours, add bullet points and check spelling (always triple-check your spelling!). Avoid using too many different styles and colours as buyers find this off-putting, and don't use too many capital letters as buyers view this as confrontational. Avoid writing threats or demands within your listing—remember to think like a retailer, no matter what it is you're selling, and make your listing as appealing as possible while remaining accurate. If there are any flaws in your product, clearly specify them here. You can create a more detailed and advanced design by clicking on the *HTML* tab at the top of this section (there is more information on HTML in part IV).

You have the option of adding one of eBay's themes in the Listing designer section (this adds a colourful border around your entire listing), and a visitor counter so you can see how many people have viewed your item.

Step 6: choose selling format

Next choose how you would like to sell your product—by auction, fixed price or a combination of both (see figure 12.7). In this example we've chosen to start the auction at 99c but have also added a Buy it now price of $3.50. If anyone bids, the Buy it now price will disappear; if no bids are placed, buyers will have the option of purchasing right away at $3.50. It's a good idea to add a Buy it now price to your auctions to appeal to as many buyers as possible while also setting a price guide for potential bidders.

Figure 12.7: step 6 of the Sell your item form

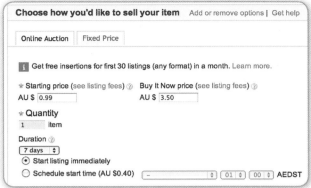

Some eBay sites allow you to set a reserve price for auctions—that is, a minimum bid amount required before the product may be bought. eBay Australia does not allow reserves except on listings for vehicles. There are two other format options: Classified, available on some eBay sites, is a straightforward advertisement on eBay requiring the buyer to contact you to arrange viewings of the product and payment; this is a non-transactional format available on eBay Australia only for vehicles, services and real estate. You can choose the other format option, Best offer, by checking the box under the Buy it now price you enter for fixed price listings. Once checked, you'll then have the option of automatically accepting or rejecting offers above or below your desired price.

We've chosen seven days for this listing—always choose a minimum of seven days so you get at least one weekend's worth of shoppers. You also have the option here of scheduling your listing. Whatever time you create your listing is the same time that it will end (after your chosen number of days), so if you're up late at night creating the listing, only other night owls will be around to bid on an auction ending at that time. Use scheduling if you want to optimise the number of shoppers on the site—aim for business hours or at least before around 9 pm.

Step 7: choose payment method

Now we need to choose how we would like to be paid for the item (see figure 12.8, overleaf). For more information on each option, see chapter 7.

In this example we have chosen to accept PayPal and bank deposit. Check the relevant boxes for the payment methods you accept. Note that if you're accepting bank deposit it's a good idea to check the 'Show buyers your bank account number in checkout' box as this will save time and make it easier for your buyers to pay you.

Figure 12.8: step 7 of the Sell your item form

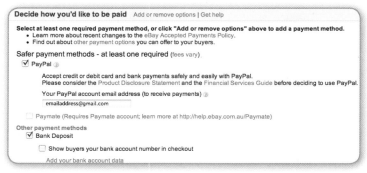

Step 8: enter postage/shipping details

Next tell your buyers about postage/shipping (see figure 12.9). Specify your postage costs and services by choosing from the drop-down lists. Note that you can also check the 'Free postage' box and not charge your buyers anything. Some sellers incorporate the cost of shipping into the item price so buyers don't have to pay extra during checkout.

Figure 12.9: step 8 of the Sell your item form

Consider using Australia Post's eBay-branded options, which are less expensive than off-the-shelf products. For more information, hover your mouse over Sell at the top of the eBay homepage then click Postage centre. If you're happy for buyers to collect from you, choose the 'Local pickup' option then specify how many handling days you will need to ship the product. If you're willing to send the product to overseas destinations, specify postage in the International postage section. You can exclude certain locations by clicking Create exclusion list.

Step 9: list your item

In the final step of this page, you can block certain buyers from purchasing your product (only do this if you have enough eBay selling experience and are sure you want to exclude certain buyers. Click Add or remove options for this functionality.) and specify a returns policy (you don't need to accept returns, but you do need to specify this from the drop-down list). You also have the option of adding any specific checkout instructions for your buyers (see figure 12.10). Click *Continue*.

Figure 12.10: step 9 of the Sell your item form

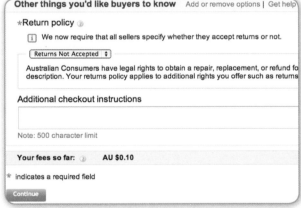

The final page is a summary of your listing, complete with fee estimates and the option of adding upgrades to help your listing stand out on the search results page. After carefully reviewing the information, click *List your item* at the bottom of the page or Edit listing if you need to change anything.

Congratulations, you've now listed a product for sale on eBay.

Listing an item for sale

Finding help

Throughout the selling form, keep a lookout for question marks (?) and Get help links—these will show you more information about that feature or give you instant access to an eBay customer service representative who will be able to help guide you through the listing process.

The Simple selling form

eBay has launched its Simple selling form on a number of sites and Australia is scheduled to receive it sometime during 2013. This form is aimed at new sellers and streamlines the listing process considerably. The US version is included here by way of example, but the Australian version is likely to be very similar. Keep watching the Australian site for announcements about this new, faster, easier way to list items.

Let's complete a listing together using the new selling form. In this example we will list a packet of tomato seeds, just as we did when using the Sell your item form earlier in this chapter.

Complete the Simple selling form

First, enter a few keywords describing what you're listing (see figure 12.11). In this example we again chose 'tomato seeds'. Click **Go**.

Figure 12.11: starting the Simple selling form

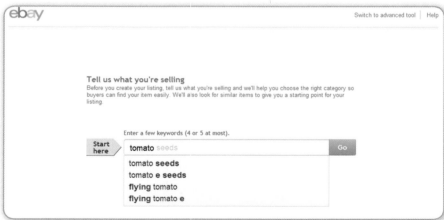

Choose the category to list your product in (we chose 'Seeds & bulbs'—see figure 12.12) then click *Create your listing*. Alternatively, click Create your listing from a similar item to recreate a listing similar to an existing listing from other sellers on eBay, which will automatically fill in some of the information for you.

Figure 12.12: choosing a category in the Simple selling form

Now you're in the Describe it section of the form (see figure 12.13, overleaf). Complete your title using a combination of strong and relevant product keywords. Click the + sign to upload a photograph from your computer.

Click Show item specifics to include relevant product information as per the example in the Sell your item form earlier in this chapter.

Complete a detailed product description under the 'Add more details' heading then click *Next*.

Don't skimp on the information

While listing using the Simple selling form will take you a shorter amount of time than using the Sell your item form, don't be tempted to skimp on essential information about the product you're selling. Some sellers find it easier to write their listing in a Word document and then simply cut and paste the information into the form when they're ready to list. Whether you list on the website or using an eBay app (covered later in this chapter), always include as much product information as possible so you appeal to more buyers and increase your chances of attracting the highest selling price.

Figure 12.13: the Describe it page of the Simple selling form

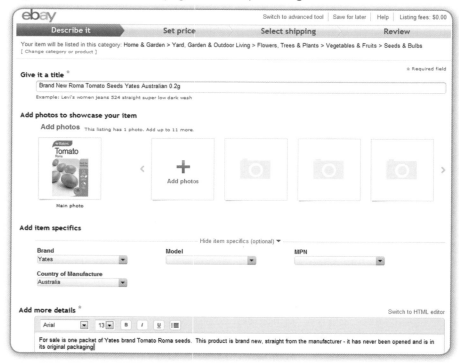

Now you're in the 'Set Price' section of the form (see figure 12.14). For auctions, enter your starting price and check the 'Add a Buy it now ...' box to include a fixed price with your auction (as outlined earlier in this chapter). In this example, as before, we started the auction at 99c with a Buy it now price of $3.50. Alternatively, click <u>Fixed price</u> at the top of the form to create a Buy it now listing (not an auction).

Choose the duration of your listing and whether you want to start the listing now or schedule it for later. In this example we chose seven days. Click *Next*.

Figure 12.14: the Set price page of the Simple selling form

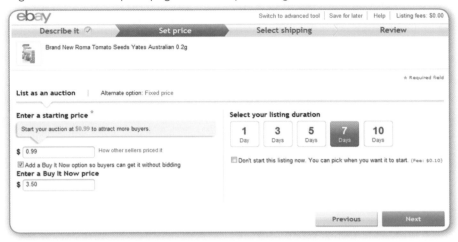

Now you're in the 'Select shipping' section of the form (see figure 12.15). Choose your preferred shipping method plus the price you will charge buyers (if any; for free shipping, check the 'Offer free shipping' box). To add multiple shipping options click Add another shipping option, and to add an international shipping option check the relevant box and complete the details of your shipping to international destinations. In this example, we chose economy domestic shipping and offered it for free. You can also click How other sellers shipped this item to gauge average shipping prices and most popular options used by other sellers in this category, or click Calculate actual cost to enter your product's dimensions and weight so buyers can calculate their own shipping costs. Click **Next**.

Figure 12.15: the Select shipping page of the Simple selling form

Finally, you're in the 'Review' section of the form (see figure 12.16). Carefully review all of the information in your listing and click <u>Edit</u> next to any section to make changes. When you're satisfied with all aspects of your listing, click *List it*.

Figure 12.16: the Review page of the simple Selling form

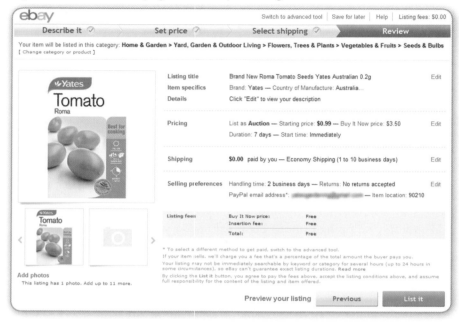

That's it! Your listing is now live on eBay.

Sell via the iPhone App

Listing an item using the iPhone app is one of the easiest and fastest ways to sell on eBay. More and more people love the convenience and speed of listing this way, and your listing appears on the eBay site the same way it would if you had used the selling form on the website.

To begin selling, click the <u>Sell</u> link at the bottom of the app screen. Here you can try scanning a barcode, or enter the information manually. Scanning a product's barcode will access eBay's product catalogue. Not all products are included yet but more are being added regularly. For more information see later in this chapter.

Click each of the relevant areas to add that information to your listing. Let's complete the steps together.

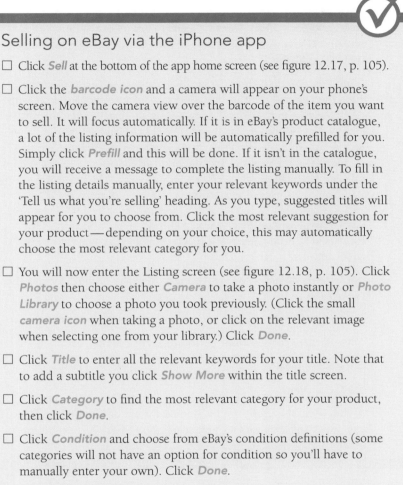

Selling on eBay via the iPhone app

☐ Click *Sell* at the bottom of the app home screen (see figure 12.17, p. 105).

☐ Click the *barcode icon* and a camera will appear on your phone's screen. Move the camera view over the barcode of the item you want to sell. It will focus automatically. If it is in eBay's product catalogue, a lot of the listing information will be automatically prefilled for you. Simply click *Prefill* and this will be done. If it isn't in the catalogue, you will receive a message to complete the listing manually. To fill in the listing details manually, enter your relevant keywords under the 'Tell us what you're selling' heading. As you type, suggested titles will appear for you to choose from. Click the most relevant suggestion for your product—depending on your choice, this may automatically choose the most relevant category for you.

☐ You will now enter the Listing screen (see figure 12.18, p. 105). Click *Photos* then choose either *Camera* to take a photo instantly or *Photo Library* to choose a photo you took previously. (Click the small *camera icon* when taking a photo, or click on the relevant image when selecting one from your library.) Click *Done*.

☐ Click *Title* to enter all the relevant keywords for your title. Note that to add a subtitle you click *Show More* within the title screen.

☐ Click *Category* to find the most relevant category for your product, then click *Done*.

☐ Click *Condition* and choose from eBay's condition definitions (some categories will not have an option for condition so you'll have to manually enter your own). Click *Done*.

☐ Click *Details* to enter product information.

☐ Click *Description* then enter the detailed listing information (as outlined in the Sell your item form example earlier in this chapter). Click *Done*.

☐ Click *Item Specifics* to enter as many key product features as possible, and when finished click *Done*.

(continued)

Listing an item for sale

Selling on eBay via the iPhone app *(cont'd)*

☐ Click *Done* (again) to return to the main listing screen.

☐ Click *Format & Price* then choose the selling format and your start price, and click *Show More* to specify your listing duration and schedule if you want your listing to start (and end) at a particular time. Click *Done*.

☐ Click *Postage* then *Destination* then *Domestic*. Click *Shipment Type* then choose your option (flat rate, calculated or local pick-up). Click *Service* and choose the postage methods you offer. Finally, enter your postage cost or choose to offer free shipping. Click *Done*. Repeat for additional services or international destinations, or to exclude selected locations by clicking *Add Shipping Service*. When finished click *Done*.

☐ Click *Preferences*.

☐ Click *Payment* then *Method* then choose your options from the list provided. Click *Payment*. If accepting PayPal, enter your PayPal email address then click *Done*.

☐ Click *Item Location*, specify the location of the product for sale then click *Done*.

☐ Click *Handling Time*, choose your option then click *Preferences*.

☐ Click *Returns*, choose your option then click *Done*.

☐ Click *Done* (again).

☐ Click *Continue*.

☐ Review all of the product and listing information carefully and once you are satisfied that it's accurate click the *Publish Listing* button at the bottom of the screen.

That's it! Your listing is now live. Next time you use the app to list another item some of this information will be stored so you do not need to enter it again. Lots of great listing tips can be found by clicking *Help* in the top right of the listing screen.

Figure 12.17: the eBay iPhone app Sell an item screen

Figure 12.18: creating your listing on the iPhone app

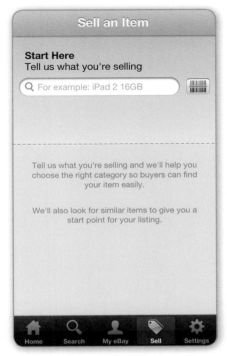

Sell via the iPad app

Selling via the iPad app is very similar to selling using the iPhone app, but let's go through the steps together. Using the iPad is even faster than using the iPhone, and you should be able to complete your listing within a few minutes (see figure 12.19, overleaf). The ticks next to each step of the listing process will change from grey to light blue once you have completed them.

Figure 12.19: the eBay iPad app Sell an item screen

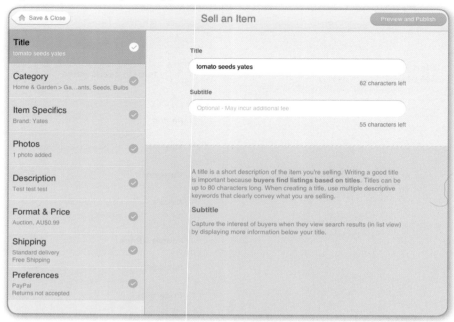

Selling on eBay via the iPad app

☐ Access the selling form by expanding the left navigation then click Sell an item.

☐ You can scan a barcode to see whether the product is listed in eBay's product catalogue. Click the barcode icon and a camera will appear on your screen. Move the camera view over the barcode of the product you wish to sell. It will focus automatically. If there is no match in the catalogue, a message will appear. If there is a match, the app will automatically prefill a lot of the listing information for you. Otherwise, complete the listing information manually.

☐ Enter your relevant keywords under the 'Tell us what you're selling' heading. As you type, suggested titles will appear for you to choose from. Click the most relevant suggestion for your product—depending on your choice, this may automatically choose the most relevant category for you.

Selling on eBay via the iPad app

☐ Click *Title* to enter all the relevant keywords for your title. You can also add a subtitle here.

☐ Click *Category* then *Choose a category* to choose the most relevant category for your product. Click *Select*.

☐ Click *Item Specifics* then *Enter item specifics* to choose from eBay's predefined options then click *Done*.

☐ Click *Photos* then the camera shutter icon. Choose either *Camera* to take a photo instantly or *Photo library* to choose from a photo you took previously. (Click the small camera icon when taking a photo, or click on the relevant image from your library then *Use*.) Repeat the process to add up to 12 photos for no additional charge.

☐ Click *Description* to add your detailed product information as outlined previously in this chapter.

☐ Click *Format & price* then choose the selling format and your start price, and click *More auction/Fixed price options* to specify your listing duration and schedule if you want your listing to start (and end) at a particular time.

☐ Click *Shipping* then *Add shipping service* then *Destination*. Choose *Domestic* or *International*, then choose a *Shipment type* from eBay's list of rates to charge your buyer. Click *Service* and choose a shipping option. Choose *Free shipping* by sliding the button to ON, or else specify your shipping cost in the field provided. Click *Done*. Click *Add shipping service* and repeat the process to give buyers additional domestic and/or international options.

☐ Click *Preferences*.

☐ Click *Payment* then choose your options from the list provided. Click *Select*. If accepting PayPal, enter your PayPal email address in the field provided. You can require immediate payment (which means your product will not be marked as sold unless a buyer pays for it) by sliding the button next to *Immediate payment* to ON.

☐ Click *Handling time* and choose your option.

☐ Click *Item location* and specify the location of the product for sale.

(continued)

Selling on eBay via the iPad app *(cont'd)*

☐ Slide the button next to *Returns* to ON to accept returns.

☐ Click the *Preview and publish* button at top right of the listing screen (or *Save & close* to return to your draft at a later date).

☐ Carefully review the listing information (click *Edit listing* to make any changes) and once you're satisfied with it, click the blue *Publish* button (to close the preview pane, click anywhere on the iPad screen outside the preview pane).

That's it! Your listing is now live. Note that the iPad app will automatically save a lot of this information and prefill your next listing with details such as payment, item location and shipping options. You can choose to keep these the same or edit as you create your next listing. Handy hints appear within each section of the listing form to help you optimise for selling success.

List a product using eBay's catalogue

Outlined earlier for the standard and simple selling forms, we chose an example of a product that is not included in eBay's catalogue. eBay is compiling a catalogue of common retail products, and stores' images and standard product information about each. Incorporating the catalogue information makes it faster to list an item and makes your listing appear more professional. It utilises the same technology as used when scanning a barcode to list your item via an eBay app.

To access the catalogue on eBay's website, rather than entering product keywords in step 1 of the Sell your item form, enter a product number (usually the barcode number found on the product or its packaging). Note that some keywords and categories will automatically access eBay's product catalogue. The catalogue will prompt you to enter the brand, product type or model. After searching the catalogue, next to the product that is exactly the same as the one you intend to sell, and click *Sell yours*. eBay will automatically add a product image, create an item title, choose your category and include detailed product information in your listing description.

More products are being added to eBay's catalogue on a regular basis; it's always a good idea to check whether your product is included, as this feature saves considerable time and effort when listing. For some categories it is mandatory to use the catalogue where there is a matching product.

The New eBay

Sell one like this

Another way to list an item for sale on eBay is to use the <u>Sell it yourself</u> link or access your previously purchased items via My eBay (as covered in chapter 8). Rather than starting your listing from scratch, conduct a search on eBay to find similar items. Once you've found one identical to yours, go to the View item page and click the <u>Sell it yourself</u> link beneath the product image. You can also access this feature from a completed listings search—click <u>Sell one like this</u> next to the item in the search results page. From your Purchase history page in My eBay, click <u>More actions</u> then <u>Sell this item</u>.

Choosing one of these options will save you time and effort by automatically completing part of the listing information for you.

Instant Sale

A brand new option for selling available on the US and UK eBay sites is called Instant Sale. For this, search a product catalogue for your specific product and see whether a third party is interested in buying it from you instantly. You'll get a cash offer, the third party will send you a pre-paid package to post the product to them and once it's received you'll be paid via PayPal. It's that simple—you don't have to deal with buyers, worry about postage or payment, or pay eBay or PayPal additional fees.

The price you get for your product tends to be slightly less than you would achieve by selling it yourself, but if you're after a fast, convenient and instant transaction, this is the selling method for you. Keep watching eBay Australia for details of Instant Sale's launch here. You will be able to access it by hovering your mouse over <u>Sell</u> at the top of the eBay homepage, then clicking <u>Check for instant offers</u>.

Chapter 13

Keeping track of listings using My eBay

Once your listing is live on the site, you can track its progress from My eBay. As covered in chapter 8, My eBay stores all your buying information, but it's also where every one of your listings and their current status is displayed. To access listing information in My eBay, hover your mouse over <u>My eBay</u> at the top of the eBay homepage then click <u>Selling/sold</u>. Let's take a closer look at the features of the selling/sold pages.

All Selling view

The default landing page for selling in My eBay is the All selling page (see figure 13.1, overleaf). In essence, it summarises all of your selling activity on one page. Starting at the top of the page, first you will see if you have any Cases in the eBay resolution centre. This is where buyers will alert eBay if they have not received an item or if an item received is not as described, or where you can alert eBay to the fact that a buyer has not paid so you can recoup your final value fee (where applicable). For more information on this, see chapter 14. In this example you can see that I have one case open and it is awaiting the buyer's response. Clicking on any link, such as <u>1 case</u>, will take you to the details of that transaction in eBay's resolution centre and give you options for responding to a buyer's claims.

Figure 13.1: the My eBay All selling page

Next on the page is a list of Selling reminders—a summary of outstanding activities. In order of summary, it outlines: buyer questions requiring an answer, sold listings awaiting payment, paid listings awaiting shipment, listings ending today and transactions requiring feedback to be left for buyers. You can click on any of the links, such as 5 items, to view those listings. At the right end of the grey Selling reminders header bar will be the Edit link and two arrows. Clicking Edit allows you to change the colour of the header bar; clicking the up or down arrows allows you to move this summary up or down the page.

If you've scheduled any listings to begin in the future, these will be listed next on the page.

Beneath scheduled listings is the Active selling header bar. Here any listing you currently have live on eBay will be listed. Clicking the links beneath the header bar will show you the corresponding listings:

- All—all active listings.

- Awaiting answer—listings with questions from buyers that you have not answered. Note that you need to have responded to questions *from* this page to mark them as answered. If you respond via Messages in My eBay they may not be marked as answered on this summary page.

- Open offers—if you accept offers on your listings, any made by buyers will appear here.

- Bids/reserve met—auction listings that have received any bids (note that eBay Australia does not allow sellers to set a reserve price, or minimum highest bid amount for auctions).

- Without bids/Reserve not met—all other listings.

- Leads—applies only to classifieds listings.

- Price markdown—applies only to sellers who use a special price reduction feature within eBay stores (for more information see part IV).

- Free shipping markdown—applies if you have reduced the cost of shipping to zero during the course of the listing

- In lists (click the small blue arrow to reveal)—listings you have added to a specific list.

You can also filter the listings that appear beneath the Active selling header using the drop-downs for Format, Sort by or Store category (if you have an eBay store). Beneath these are several action buttons that can be applied to any listing by checking the empty box next to each item title. You can also perform these actions for multiple listings by checking more than one box, or for all listings by checking the box at the top of the section next to the *Add note* button. The buttons are:

- *Add note*—allows you to write yourself a note (not visible to buyers) about the product in this listing (for example, how much it cost you originally, or the name and phone number of someone coming to view the product)

- *Edit*—allows you to make certain edits to the actual listing

- *Send to online auction*—if you have a *Buy it now* listing, allows you to change to auction format (note this will prompt you to relist as fixed price if you originally listed it as an auction)

- *Add to list*—allows you to create a collection of specific listings (for example, all those where local pick-up is offered)

- *End*—will end a listing immediately.

Beneath these buttons are the actual listings. The listing title can be clicked to take you through to the View item page. If you have unanswered questions, the number can be clicked to view the buyer's question. The columns to the right are: Views/Watchers, Bids (for auctions), Price and Time left. You can click on any of these links to reorder the listings by this information (lowest to highest or vice versa). The final column is Actions. Here you have several options.

- Respond — reply to answer buyers' questions

- Send to online auction — if your listing is fixed price and did not sell, you have the option to relist it as an auction (or relist as fixed price if it was auction)

- Sell similar — some of the listing information will be pre-populated for you

- Revise — edit a live listing

- Add to description — add a footnote to your live listing to include information you may have forgotten to add

- End item — ends the listing

- Add note — add a note to the listing that buyers cannot see

- Add to list — create a collection of listings with specific conditions (such as all local pick-up)

Further down the page in the All selling summary you will see Sold listings (see figure 13.2). This is probably the most important part of selling within My eBay. Here you can monitor the status of each of your sold items.

Figure 13.2: the My eBay Sold page

The links at the top of the section are:

- <u>All</u>—see all sold listings
- <u>Awaiting answer</u>—see sold listings with questions from buyers that require answering
- <u>Awaiting total</u>—the buyer has requested the total amount to be paid
- <u>Awaiting payment</u>—the item has sold but the buyer has not yet paid
- <u>Awaiting shipment</u>—you have yet to mark the product as shipped
- <u>Awaiting feedback</u>—the buyer has not yet left feedback for the transaction
- <u>Shipped</u>—products you have marked as shipped
- <u>In lists</u>—sold items you have added to a list that you created.

Beneath these links you can change the time period of sold listings you'd like to view by using the drop-down next to 'Period' and on the right change the sorting order next to 'Sort by'.

Listings appear next. Check the empty box next to the listing to use one of the action buttons at the bottom of the section:

- <u>Delete</u>—removes the listing from your sold list (only do so after all actions have been completed)
- <u>Print shipping labels</u> (coming soon to eBay Australia)—allows you to print labels to adhere to packages you send. You are automatically billed by shipping providers via your PayPal account.
- <u>Relist</u>—sends the same listing live again for sale (helpful if the buyer does not pay or you have more than one of the same product for sale)
- <u>Add note</u>—adds a note to the sold listing that the buyer cannot see
- <u>Add tracking number</u>—if you use a tracked shipping method you can upload a tracking number here so buyers can trace the status of their own package
- <u>Add to list</u>—create lists of sold products for your own reference.

You can click the item title to go through to the completed View item page of the product. Clicking on the buyer's user ID will take you to their My world page and you can click on their feedback score to see their feedback profile (see chapter 1). Click Add beneath these to upload a tracking number (if applicable).

To the right of the listings are the status columns. Click 'Price' or 'Sale date' to reorder the list by this information. The five icons that appear to the right of these columns are:

- *Calculator.* The buyer has completed checkout.

- *Dollar sign.* The buyer has paid for the product (note that this automatically changes colour if payment has been made via PayPal).

- *Envelope.* You have marked the product as shipped.

- *Pencil.* You have left feedback for the buyer for this transaction.

- *Star.* You have received feedback from the buyer.

Some of these icons will automatically change from grey to blue once the action has been completed. For others, you may need to manually mark the action as completed. You can do this by choosing an action from the column on the far right:

- Print shipping label — this is covered in chapter 31

- Send invoice — creates a total amount owing invoice for buyers and sends this to them via email

- Leave feedback — leave a feedback rating for your buyer

- Add tracking number — as covered previously in this chapter

- Mark as shipped — mark the product as shipped (this notifies the buyer that the item is on its way)

- View order details — takes you to a summary of the order (receipts can be printed from this page)

- View PayPal transaction — takes you to PayPal to view the transaction and whether the payment has been processed (if paid via PayPal)

- Contact buyer — send the buyer a message

- Unmark as payment received — change from paid to unpaid

- <u>Sell similar</u>—creates a new listing with some of the information prefilled for you

- <u>Relist as fixed price</u>—sends the listing live again for resale

- <u>Add note</u>—as covered previously in this chapter

- <u>Add to list</u>—as covered previously in this chapter

- <u>Report this buyer</u>—alerts eBay to buyer behaviour that is outside of policy (for example, made unreasonable demands, misused the returns process or other problems).

Beneath the Sold list is the Returns list. Coming soon to eBay Australia, sellers will be able to offer a returns procedure via eBay, and this is where they will be notified of the status of any returned items.

Unsold items appear next in the summary. From here you can relist your products to try selling them again.

Deleted items will appear towards the bottom of the summary. Any listing you have deleted from one of the summary views will be displayed here so you can take actions against that listing.

Importantly, Announcements from eBay appear at the very bottom of the page. These announcements may affect your selling experience so it's a good idea to check for them regularly. Listing offers may also appear at the bottom of the summary page, where from time to time eBay offers discounted listing fees.

Note that you can also access each of these lists by clicking the relevant link under the 'Sell' heading in the navigation area on the left of My eBay.

For iPhone, click on the <u>My eBay</u> link at the bottom of the app home screen then click *Selling* to access most of these features, or simply click the *Selling* button on the home screen.

For iPad, click the *Selling* button on the home screen, or access the left navigation and click <u>Selling</u> under My eBay.

Keeping track of listings using My eBay

Chapter 14
Accepting payments

As covered in chapter 7, there are a variety of payment methods you can accept as an eBay seller. When you're receiving payments, it's always a good idea to ensure the money has cleared into your relevant account before you send the product to the buyer. If there are any delays, you should communicate this to your buyer to set realistic expectations.

PayPal

PayPal, an eBay company, is one of the safest ways to accept payments when you sell items on eBay. Not only does it offer buyers peace of mind through its buyer protection scheme (which may cover buyers for up to $20 000), but it also means you as the seller need never share your bank or other financial details—all exchanges of funds are activated by revealing only your email address.

When a buyer pays with PayPal, the sold listing will automatically be marked as paid. You can also check your balance by logging directly into PayPal (at www.paypal.com.au) and clicking My account then Overview or History. Here you will see a list of all payments received and you can click Details to see more information about the transaction.

While your customers' eBay and Paypal address should be the same, it's always a good idea to ensure you send your products to the address your buyer enters as part of eBay checkout. To qualify for PayPal Seller protection sellers must post the item to the address the customer provides during checkout. To see more information about PayPal's Seller protection scheme, click *Personal* at the top of any PayPal screen then click Sell then More about security.

Be aware that some PayPal payments are delayed because the buyer is funding via their bank account and does not have a backup funding source. These are known as eCheque payments. The delay is usually between three and seven working days, depending on how long it takes the relevant financial institution to clear payment. Always wait for PayPal to inform you that payment has cleared before sending your products, and for any lengthy delays keep your buyer informed of the progress.

Accepting payment via PayPal does attract a small fee (refer to chapter 17 for more on eBay and PayPal fees).

Bank deposits

It costs you nothing to accept deposits from buyers into your bank account. If you're accepting bank transfers, it's a good idea to include your bank account number within checkout so buyers can access it immediately. You add your number in the payments section of the Sell your item form. To pay you, a buyer logs into their internet banking account and completes a funds transfer or else visits a branch of your bank and deposits the money directly into your account.

Note that payments made over the counter cannot have a reference number attached to them so your buyer will not be able to identify themselves with a payment; internet transfers do have this functionality, so it's a good idea to encourage your buyers to complete the transaction online and specify their eBay user ID as reference. This will make it much easier for you to track bank payments (by logging into your bank account online and looking for deposits). If you're selling multiple items of similar or equal value it can be very difficult to match payments to buyers, so exercise caution when listing large quantities of products.

Cash

If you allow buyers to collect the item from you, most will ask if they can pay cash on pick-up. As it's impossible to track cash payments, it's a sensible idea to purchase an inexpensive invoice book from your local newsagent or stationer and write a receipt for the buyer to sign. These books cost only a few dollars and give both you and the buyer additional peace of mind. You can sign the receipt to say cash has been paid and the buyer should sign the receipt to say the goods have been collected. While this receipt won't cover you for any eBay or PayPal protection, it could serve as evidence in the unlikely event of a dispute over payment.

Money transfers

Money transfers, such as those offered by Western Union and MoneyGram, are banned on eBay. You cannot ask buyers to pay via these mechanisms, and you should refuse a buyer's request to do so. Transfers cannot be traced or reversed.

Cheques and money orders

If you elect to accept cheques and money orders, clearly set your buyer's expectations by stating that it can take up to seven working days for the funds to appear in your bank account. Of course, accepting these methods of payment means the additional effort of going to your local financial institution to cash or bank the cheque. Always wait for the funds to clear before sending your products or allowing them to be collected.

Paymate

Paymate is an Australian company offering a similar service to PayPal. You don't need to register to use Paymate, however, as each transaction is performed as a one-off transfer of funds. Buyers need to enter their credit card or bank details for each payment and the funds appear in the seller's nominated account or credit card. The only information exchanged between buyer and seller is an email address. Paymate keeps the financial information secure. Its standard fee rate is 2.475 per cent plus 55c per transaction.

Paymate also has a fraud protection scheme for sellers; more information can be found on the Paymate website at www.paymate.com.au.

Credit card

You, or a business you own, may have merchant credit card processing capabilities. You can offer buyers the option of paying for their products by credit card; however, credit card payment is not integrated into eBay. You need to communicate with the buyer to receive their credit details, which you can enter into your merchant facility manually.

Processing credit cards attracts a small fee from your financial institution, and this can vary depending on the type of card used. Some banks and other institutions also offer merchants protection against chargebacks and fraud—contact your provider for further details.

Chapter 15
Postage and handling tips

It's standard procedure on eBay not to send your products until payment for the item has cleared. Once payment has been received and processed, take the time to offer great service through the postage, handling and packaging methods you use.

Free postage

A common e-commerce standard is offering free shipping or postage. It has become so common, in fact, that some buyers have come to expect it. But while it's all well and good for a business seller to absorb postage costs within a product's sale price, for us private sellers it can be more difficult to provide free postage. The secret here is to be certain what the postage costs will be. I've seen too many casual sellers make the mistake of estimating their postage inaccurately and ending up forfeiting most of their profit because they quoted the wrong amount. If you're prepared to send an item via the post or courier, get clear estimates from your shipping provider (visit the Australia Post website at www.auspost.com.au for postage estimates).

Here's a handy little tip for helping with your selling success. Once you know your postage costs, consider increasing the auction start price or your Buy it now price to cover the postage costs, then offer 'free' postage. You'll be surprised how much buyers love the idea that anything comes for free!

Postage options

Other buyers, however, are prepared to pay reasonable postage costs, so again ensure you have an accurate guide to avoid surprising buyers with a high delivery fee at the end of the listing. It's a good idea to offer your buyers a few options for postage (standard and express, for example), and if you're selling a more expensive item it's sensible to offer (or automatically provide) registered or insured postage options.

If you plan on selling regularly, get to know your local Australia Post staff as most are familiar with selling on eBay and should be able to provide you with the best advice for getting your products safely and cost-effectively to both domestic and international destinations. Australia Post also sells pre-paid eBay satchels and boxes at a cheaper rate than paying for standard products off the shelf. You can find more information by hovering your mouse over Sell at the top of the eBay homepage and clicking Postage centre. On this page you'll also find a postage calculator, a postcode finder and a currency converter, and information about couriers.

Posting products internationally may attract quarantine or import duties for the buyer. If you think this might be the case, clearly state within your listing that paying these charges is the buyer's responsibility.

Couriers

Larger items should generally be sent via a courier (Australia Post has a size and weight restriction on packages). Some sellers give their postcode in their listing so buyers can contact their preferred courier, but a better service option is to get a quote from a courier company and include this in your listing information. You will need to provide a list of destinations (such as east coast, South Australia or Western Australia) with corresponding costs, or you could provide a link to your preferred courier's website so buyers can obtain their own estimate and make an informed decision before purchasing your product.

You could also offer to deliver the product yourself within a specified delivery area. Bear in mind that the petrol costs and wear and tear on your vehicle should be factored in and that some buyers may not think it's fair to pay for delivery from a non-professional company. Discuss all options with your buyer and arrive at a mutually agreeable outcome.

Local pick-up

Offering local pick-up is another way of simplifying your selling experience. Be clear in your listing details about where the product is located (give buyers a rough guide to where you are so they can calculate estimated travelling time, such as 'the product can be picked up from Glebe, a five-minute drive west of the Sydney CBD') and outline when it can be picked up (days and hours are preferable).

If you're offering local pick-up, be prepared to be flexible! I've had last-minute cancellations and 11 pm phone calls to rearrange pick-up. While this is generally out of the ordinary, always be courteous to your buyer and stick to the payment methods you've specified in your listing. A 'side deal' offering cash outside of the eBay system may result in your being out of pocket if there's no proof the buyer has collected the product from you.

Some sellers charge a fee for local pick-up to cover the labour costs of getting the product into the buyer's vehicle. While a minority of internet sellers insist on this charge, buyers tend to avoid products that attract this fee so think carefully before charging buyers for local pick-up.

Handling time

It's mandatory to specify the anticipated handling time within your eBay listing. The longer it takes for you to get the product to the post office or courier, the less interested buyers are likely to be. A good guide is to specify a handling time of three days or less and ensure you stick to your guide to avoid buyer disappointment.

If a delay in shipping the product is likely, clearly specify this in your listing and handling time. It's much better to be honest with your buyers and set realistic expectations than ambush them with a lengthy delay after they have already paid.

Packaging

One of the most important aspects of being a successful eBay seller is ensuring the product is delivered into the buyer's hands safely. It's tempting to use old or damaged boxes or bags that are lying around the house to package your products, but this will likely increase the risk of damage in transit. If you're sending fragile items, take special care to protect them. If you need to use specialised packaging, factor these costs into your selling price and outline to your buyers that extra care is taken to get the product to them in good condition—added buyer confidence can lead to premium selling prices or faster sales.

A good packing option is to recycle paper by shredding it and packing it around the product in a sturdy box. Australia Post products such as padded bags and boxes are designed to help protect items during transit, or you could consider bulk-buying packaging products on eBay.

Optional extras

Even if selling only a handful of products each year, some sellers add that special touch by including a personalised thank-you note when they send packages. Business sellers often include information about their other eBay listings, or links to their eBay store (see part IV). You may also include inexpensive extras in the package, such as a bookmark for books, or a DVD cleaning cloth when you sell a movie. Little touches like this help make the eBay experience special and impress buyers, who may then respond by leaving you very positive feedback and ratings—both of which will benefit your future eBay selling experience.

Chapter 16
Customer service

Even if you sell only one or two items a year on eBay, you still need to know a thing or two about customer service. Buyers aren't just looking for a great deal or a professional listing; they also want to know they're dealing with a professional person who will respond to their needs as a buyer. Sellers who think it's not important to treat their buyers like retail customers will quickly find they aren't getting bids on their auctions, or that the prices they're able to achieve fall well below expectations. Throughout part III of this book I have reminded you to *keep thinking like a retailer*, and this extends to customer service.

Remember that your buyers are more than likely buying a product they have never seen from someone they have never met. Buyers also generally part with their money before they receive their products, so the buyer most often carries the risk. Reassuring potential buyers that you are genuine and professional will increase your chances of a successful and profitable selling experience on eBay.

Be professional and courteous

Customer service begins with your product listing. Both the language you use and the design contribute to a prospective buyer's overall impression of your level of service. Make sure your listing does not contain spelling errors, avoid aggressive or forceful language, and stay away from capital letters and exclamation marks (which come across as shouting to online shoppers). Similarly, your product photo must be as professional as possible. Avoid overdesigning your listing by using too many fonts, colours, flashing images or text, and stay away from dark backgrounds and fonts that are difficult to read.

Sometimes a buyer will ask you a question, and perhaps the answer is already clearly stated in your listing. This doesn't mean your buyer is stupid. They may have been in a hurry when they read your description, or perhaps the way you have worded it means it is not as clear to them as it sounds to you. Always respond to buyer questions in an efficient and respectful manner — you never know, this may be the person who intends spending the most on your product. Respond to emails as quickly as you can, preferably within 24 hours (which means when you have a listing on the site you should check your email or eBay's My messages at least once per day).

It's also a good idea to let your buyers know when you've posted or shipped the item. This sets a clear expectation in your buyer's mind and will mean they can alert you if the product is not received within a reasonable time period. From time to time you may hear from a buyer that they have not received their purchase. For expensive products, it's therefore a good idea to offer registered post or shipping insurance; for less expensive products, you may wish to offer the buyer a refund, although this is entirely up to you. The vast majority of people are honest, and if you've not taken any measures to insure a product during transit, you should take responsibility in the event that it does not reach your buyer safely. This problem will arise only rarely, so offering a refund is a small price to pay for the dollars you could make by selling frequently on the site.

Remember that all your hard work providing good customer service will pay off when the buyer leaves you feedback for your selling performance and detailed seller ratings. Great reviews of your service will help you perform better as a seller because, among other factors, Best match rewards sellers with the highest ratings from buyers.

If you're unsure what great online customer service looks like, buy a few items from a range of eBay sellers and take note of the ones that go out of their way to make you feel special. Learning what *not* to do is just as valuable.

Leave feedback for your buyers

There is some debate over when is the right time to leave feedback for your buyers. (Note that you can no longer leave negative feedback for buyers.) The best thing to do is leave feedback for your buyers once they have paid for the item. In essence, this is the only responsibility of buyers on eBay — once they've paid, their job is complete and it's up to the seller to deliver the product safely into their hands.

Leave professional, courteous and friendly comments for your buyers, as they remain visible on eBay forever.

Chapter 17
eBay's selling fees

eBay's selling fees are continually evolving so make sure you check the site at http://pages.ebay.com.au/help/sell/fees.html for the most up-to-date fees. The fees also vary among eBay sites so if you're listing on a site in another country, check for local fee rates. Table 17.1 shows eBay Australia's fee table for casual, or private, sellers. If you sell in large volume or have an eBay store, your fees will likely be different from what is listed below (see part IV for more information).

Table 17.1: eBay Australia's fees for private sellers

Format (# in brackets is listing per month)		Auction and fixed price (1–40)	Auction and fixed price (40 +)
Insertion Fees	Collectables		
	$0.01–$19.99		$0.50
	$20.00–$99.99		$1.50
	$100.00 +		$3.50
	Media	$0.00	
	$0.01–$19.99		$0.50
	$20.00–$99.99		$1.50
	$100.00 +		$3.50
	Other		
	$0.01–$19.99		$0.50
	$20.00–$99.99		$1.50
	$100.00 +		$3.50
Final Value Fee	Collectables, fashion, electronics accessories, media		
	Business and industrial, home and garden, lifestyle, car parts and accessories, electronics (<$200)	9.90%	
	Electronics (> $200)		
	Cap	$250	
PayPal fees (if the buyer pays with PayPal)		2.4% (+30 c per transaction)	

Let's look at a practical example so you can see precisely what fees you would pay in a typical transaction. If I list a refrigerator for sale at $300 and it's my third listing within the month, my fees will be:

$0 Insertion + (9.9% × $300) Final value + (2.4% × $300 + 30c) PayPal fees

= $0 + $29.70 + $7.20 + $0.30 = $37.20

My total eBay and PayPal fees equal 12.4 per cent of the sale price.

eBay also offers some optional features you can use to help optimise your sales potential (remember, it's free to add up to 12 photographs per listing). You can pay the following optional feature fees:

- *Subtitle ($2)*. Add a subtitle to appear in the search results pages to include additional information for your buyers. Note that subtitle keywords are not referenced in an eBay search.

- *Add* Buy it now *price to an auction (free)*. This allows potential buyers to purchase your product instantly at a set price prior to any bids being placed at auction.

- *Schedule (free)*. Choose your listing's start time (and therefore end time) to optimise the number of buyers who may see the listing as it finishes.

- *List in two categories (doubles your insertion fees, if applicable)*. Get more exposure for your products by listing them in two categories.

Chapter 18
Troubleshooting for eBay sellers

If at any time during the listing and selling process you need help, don't hesitate to contact eBay's Customer service team. More details can be found in chapter 1.

What to do if your buyer doesn't pay

Occasionally you may experience a buyer who wins an auction or buys your product and then fails to follow through with payment. You should contact your buyer via Messages to remind them politely to pay for their product. If payment has not been received within three to seven days, however, it's unlikely the buyer is still interested. In this situation you should lodge a claim via the eBay resolution centre both for the refund of your final value fees and to alert eBay to your non-paying buyer.

Within the 'Sold' list of My eBay a link will automatically appear for Open unpaid item case/Cancel transaction to begin the claim process for qualifying (unpaid) items. eBay will send the buyer a reminder to pay and if they fail to do so will cancel the transaction on your behalf. Your final value fees will be credited to your account.

You can automate this process to begin after a specific number of days without payment. To do this, click My eBay at the top of any eBay page then click Site preferences. Under the 'Selling preferences' heading look for 'Unpaid item assistant', then click Show on the right. Click Edit to automate this process.

What to do if your item doesn't sell

Sometimes the products you list for sale may not attract any bidders or buyers. You may have asked an unrealistic price, seller competition may have beat you to the buyers, or perhaps your listing was not enticing enough. If you want to try again, there are a number of tactics you can employ:

- Lower the asking or start price.

- Change to a different format (for example, list at auction with a low start price or add a Buy it now price to your auction).

- Check the quality of your photographs, and upload more and better photos if applicable.

- Check the description information carefully. Does it contain errors? Is it confusing? Is it comprehensive enough?

- Conduct a completed items search to gauge what price similar items are selling for, and how frequently they are selling.

- Consider relisting the product on an international eBay site to expand your buyer reach.

If you pay any insertion fees for a listing, relist it and then sell it successfully, eBay will refund the insertion fees to your account, so it's well worth revisiting your listing and trying to get it sold.

What to do if you can't find your listing on eBay

Once you complete your listing, its appearance on the site may be delayed as eBay checks it for policy violations. It can take up to 24 hours for your listing to be visible to buyers. Once it is live, you're competing with every other seller for exposure in the search results pages. Best match rewards those sellers who have a proven track record of great sales and service and those products that are most relevant to any given search. New listings are awarded a number of impressions to gauge whether they can perform as well as existing listings with a track record of sales and happy customers.

Building a strong feedback score is important for ongoing sales success on eBay. If you're an infrequent seller it's advisable to stick to the auction format and add a Buy it now price, as most auctions will get exposure on the first few pages of a search result near the end of their time remaining (time ending is a factor for exposure for auction listings but not for fixed price listings).

What to do if a buyer complains

eBay was founded on the belief that people are basically good. As an eBay seller you're in the business of providing customer service, whether you like it or not! Some buyers have high expectations (or perhaps your listing has not set accurate expectations), and this can lead to disappointment. Buyers may not receive their purchase in the mail or it may be damaged in transit. The product may not operate the way it is supposed to, or perhaps it's just not what your buyer was expecting.

In most instances, the first thing a buyer will do is contact you to let you know about the problem. As a seller you have the option of providing a refund, sending another product (if you have more than one available) or fixing the fault. It's up to you whether you want the buyer to send the product back to you. This is why you should always specify a clear and fair returns policy in your eBay listing. As a private seller you're under no obligation to provide a refund; however, leaving your buyer dissatisfied may result in your receiving negative feedback or low seller ratings. This, in turn, can affect your future ability to sell on the site.

For expensive items you should take necessary precautions to protect both you and the buyer. This can include using registered or insured shipping options, accepting PayPal and complying with its Buyer and Seller protection schemes, and packaging your items safely and securely so they are protected during transit. Being clear and explicit in your item description is the best place to start. If you do receive a buyer complaint, be patient, understanding and professional in your communications to help keep the eBay community safe and active.

Basic selling TOP 10

10 things you need to know about selling products on eBay

1   Conduct a completed listings search to gauge average prices, popularity and good listing practices for you to emulate.

2   Take clear, plain and well-lit photographs of your products — images are often the main way buyers shop and are the first things they notice.

3   When you describe your item, think like a retailer — entice your buyers by being thorough, accurate and professional.

4   Use eBay's prefilled, category and item-specific information to help keep buyers informed and to optimise your listing's exposure in eBay's search results pages.

5   Accept PayPal and be aware of its Buyer and Seller protection guidelines so both you and your buyer can transact with complete peace of mind.

6   Specify shipping costs for your buyers and consider offering free postage if you can absorb the cost of shipping into the item's price.

7   Pack your products carefully and professionally to ensure they arrive safely and securely.

8   When you sell an item on eBay you're providing a customer service — for a smooth, hassle-free transaction treat your buyers with respect and professionalism.

9   Track your listings within My eBay and keep your buyers informed of their payment and shipping progress.

10 Leave encouraging feedback for buyers when they pay for their product — it makes a good first impression and sets the tone for a positive buyer experience.

PART IV

Planning your profitable eBay business (Advanced selling part I)

Questions answered in this part

Chapter 19: The foundations of a profitable business
- How do the four Ps of retail apply to my eBay business?
- How should I think of my eBay business as a distinct entity?

Chapter 20: Researching products, competitors and customers
- How do I research my industry or category?
- How can I research eBay sales?
- What do I need to know about my prospective customers?

Chapter 21: Sourcing products to sell
- How do I know if a product is right to sell on eBay?
- What are the different ways of sourcing products to sell?
- What do I need to consider for expanding my product range?

(continued)

Questions answered in this part *(cont'd)*

Chapter 22: Budgeting for profit
- How do you define gross and net profit?
- How do you calculate profit margin?
- What costs are involved in running an eBay business?

Chapter 23: Setting up your business operations
- How do I register as a business?
- How do I register a business name?
- How should my office be organised?
- How should I organise my warehouse?

Chapter 24: Your eBay brand
- How do I make my brand consistent across eBay?
- How do I make my branding relevant?
- Do I need to have my brand professionally designed?

Chapter 25: Listing your products and managing inventory
- How do I create an effective product listing?
- How can I save time listing a large amount of inventory?
- What tools are available to help me manage my inventory on eBay?
- How do I access eBay's API for bulk upload?
- What is Magento?

Chapter 26: Best match—visibility in eBay search
- How do my sales impact on my placement in search?
- How do I make my listing more relevant in searches?
- How does my performance impact on my search ranking?
- How do I improve my search ranking?

Questions answered in this part

Chapter 27: Opening a store and marketing options

- What is an eBay store?

- How can a store help improve my eBay business?

- How should I brand and design my store?

- How do I market my business on and off eBay?

Chapter 28: eBay and PayPal fees

- How do I pay my eBay fees?

- What are the fees to sell on eBay Australia?

- What are the fees to sell on other eBay sites?

- What are PayPal's fees?

- What other fees could I be charged for accepting payments?

Chapter 19
The foundations of a profitable business

At an eBay conference three years ago I asked a group of 500 sellers for show of hands on who identified as a retailer. About 10 per cent of the audience cautiously raised their hands. I went on to suggest that if the other 90 per cent didn't consider themselves retailers, they were not running their eBay businesses correctly. Whether you are new to running an eBay business, are an existing manufacturer or wholesaler, or already run a bricks-and-mortar or online retail business, you must approach your eBay business as a retailer would. The classic four Ps of retail are *product*, *place*, *price* and *promotion*. The principles of eBay selling are no different: you must choose a product that has demand on the site; you must ensure your customers can find it; when you sell it you have to maintain a reasonable profit but also sell at a price your customers like; and promoting yourself and your products will lead to a more successful business.

But more than this, you need to approach your eBay business like the most *progressive* of retailers—one prepared to meet the demands of a new kind of shopper (the online shopper), with a back-end operation in place that capitalises on some of the advantages that having an online business offers. The reality of selling on eBay is that everything you do is visible not only to your customers but also to your competitors. Having a sound strategy in place before you begin is critical for success. Being a successful retailer is all about responding to your customer's needs, and understanding the eBay customer and how you can keep them happy is another underlying tenet. An eBay business is, by definition, a customer service–oriented business. During your daily interactions with customers you will frequently need to bend over backwards to keep them happy.

On the other hand, starting an eBay business or expanding your existing operation to include an eBay channel can cost very little in upfront investment. In fact, you can be up and running in a matter of minutes, without having to spend tens of thousands of dollars building your own website, integrating merchant payment processing systems or finding ways to get noticed via internet search engines. Many existing eBay sellers seem to have 'fallen into' the business—they started out small but the demand for their products was so high that before they knew it they were turning over more than a million dollars a year. For some of them, it was too late to create new ways of operating, or they found they did not have the time to go back and make changes. I've seen some operators who are barely keeping afloat because they failed to take the time to plan carefully for future growth.

Most small business owners I talk to complain they simply do not have the time to reassess their operations because they're too busy dealing with customers and processing orders. In this part of the book I'll show you how to plan carefully for eBay success so that when it comes you won't be wasting precious time, money and resources fixing aspects of your business that should have been operating correctly from the outset.

The simplest advice I have is this: don't rush into your eBay business. You might think you know a lot about retail, resale, products or customers, but it's practically impossible to predict how your business model will cope with the potential demand until you tap into the more than 7 million Australians who visit eBay each month. Planning for future growth today is one of the best kept secrets of profitable businesses, and your eBay plan begins with this book—no, not with part IV, but with parts I to III. So if you thought you could jump straight into this section and skip the basics, think again.

The most successful eBay businesses understand exactly how buyers look for products on the site, what they assess before making a purchase and what they expect after they have parted with their funds. Understanding and having experience of the eBay selling basics are critical, too, because like all new things we need to start at the beginning before we can advance with confidence. The first thing I tried to sell on eBay was a collection of movie posters. My description was appalling, I didn't include a photograph and I didn't advise of postage costs—no wonder they never sold! That was 11 years ago, and today I'm running a highly profitable business selling to hundreds of customers every week. Even the largest sellers on eBay today (and some of them have gross sales of many millions) started out by understanding the basics, and the best way to gain that knowledge is to experience it first hand. Being an eBay buyer and a casual seller is the fastest path to running a profitable eBay business. So if you skipped it, turn back now to the beginning of the book and learn about all the basic aspects of using eBay. Take your time.

If you're already running an eBay business, part IV gives you an opportunity to critically analyse all components of your operations, to tweak and streamline your business and ensure you're operating it as profitably as possible. In the appendix of this book you will find a template for creating a comprehensive business plan. Read parts IV and V of this book first, taking any necessary notes as you proceed. Then, after you have digested all of the information, refer to the business plan and create a comprehensive outline for your business's future. Writing a detailed business plan will require patience and commitment, but planning for profit and success today will help you realise both in the medium to long term.

For education, tips and guidance on running a successful eBay business, also refer to the Seller centre. It can be accessed by hovering your mouse over Sell at the top of any eBay page, then clicking Seller centre.

Use eBay iPad and iPhone apps for business

In the previous sections of the book we covered using the eBay website via a computer and using mobile apps such as those available for iPad and iPhone. While these mobile apps are handy for eBay business owners to check daily sales or grab individual buyer details when you're away from your computer, they're not the most efficient way to operate your business's back end. In this part of the book, therefore, we'll refer to mobile apps only where there is a specific product feature that can help streamline your operations—that is, where mobile app features are more efficient than using your computer.

Chapter 20

Researching products, competitors and customers

Conducting the right research can make the difference between building a profitable eBay business and one that struggles to survive. One of the great things about eBay is that it is a transparent marketplace—that is, most of the information about products, categories and other sellers is visible for all to see. This gives you a unique opportunity to gauge the potential for your own eBay business *before* you make any investment in products or back-end operations. Conducting thorough research is the critical first step in creating a viable long-term eBay business.

Industry research

A good place to start is to research a number of industries (or categories or products) to see what information you can find online. Look for annual and other financial reports of companies that sell or manufacture the products you're most interested in selling. What are the growth figures in these industries over the past three years, and what do experts predict for the future of sales in that industry? What is happening to the average sales prices of products in the industry—are they falling or steady? (Even a rising price is not necessarily an indicator of long-term viability.) Who are the largest sellers and manufacturers in the industry, and are there any imminent local or international threats? Check out IBISWorld (www.ibisworld.com.au) or Roy Morgan (www.roymorganonlinestore.com), which release hundreds of industry reports each year. You will need to pay a subscription or per-report fee to access these evaluations. A thorough search of the Australian Bureau of Statistics website (www.abs.gov.au) can also be helpful, and most of its reports are free.

Although this may be more difficult to find, look for specific information relating to online sales of the products. Is there online demand?

You can also piece together your own research simply by conducting a few strategic internet searches. Look at who the top advertisers are on Google, and analyse their website's strengths and weaknesses. Where possible, buy from these businesses and see what opportunities there may be in treating the products or customers differently—is this achievable on eBay? Google trends (www.google.com.au/trends/) helps you understand which keywords are most searched for by users, and Alexa (www.alexa.com) will give you an indication of the levels of internet traffic to specific companies to help you gauge buyer demand.

If you still can't find information that can help you decide whether a particular product or industry has potential for internet sales, try picking up the phone and speaking to a decision maker at one of the leading companies in the industry. LinkedIn (www.linkedin.com) is a great website for identifying industry thought leaders and other valuable information.

eBay research

You'll also need to conduct thorough research on eBay to understand whether there's a viable business opportunity selling specific products on the site. The easiest place to start is to conduct a completed listings search. This will show you recent months' sold and unsold items and give you an understanding of frequency of sales and prices achieved. You can also click on listings to see various sellers' listing details, including an idea of shipping, payment and terms of trade. To access a completed listings search, click Advanced next to the *Search* button at the top of the eBay homepage then enter your product's keywords, check the 'Completed listings' box and click *Search*. In the search results, sold items, prices will appear in green text and include a small 'sold' icon, and unsold items appear in red.

For more advanced eBay research consider a tool called Terapeak (www.terapeak.com). Terapeak accesses eBay data to show you a history of sales, common search terms, top sellers and their average turnover, most popular listings, suggestions for optimal listing titles and more. The tool covers eBay Australia and most other eBay sites so you can gauge both local and international opportunities. It is the first place I look when considering new product lines to sell on eBay and to monitor my current sales performance versus that of my competitors. Access to the tool costs between $29.95 and $49.95 per month, depending on which option you choose. Sellers who take the time to use the tool properly frequently comment on its value for money.

You can also learn more about eBay success stories by attending eBay events or finding helpful sellers via eBay's discussion boards (see chapter 1 for more information).

Customer research

It's harder to find specific research about eBay's buyers, but by using a combination of eBay research and your own deductions you will be able to compile a list of must-haves for buyers of your chosen products. Look carefully at the most successful sellers in the category and read their item descriptions thoroughly. Which sellers repeatedly appear at the top of search results — that is, which sellers does Best match deem to be the best and to sell the most popular products? What kinds of keywords are repeated most frequently? Look for the following clues:

- Are the listings described primarily in terms of quality, or lowest price?

- Is complex product information explained carefully?

- Are warranties or guarantees usually provided by the top sellers?

- Are returns provided for by the top sellers? If so, how long do buyers have to return the products?

- What kind of feedback have buyers left for the sellers? Look particularly at any negative feedback, as this is a clear indicator of the types of issues you will likely face.

- Do sellers include the Best offer option — that is, are buyers likely to want to haggle over price?

- Are the top sellers presenting their listings with professional photography and well-designed listing templates, or are their designs more basic?

Asking these and other questions of established sellers in a category will help you identify customer requirements. Even if a seller does not list your specific products on eBay, there will be sellers within the category selling similar types of products.

Most important of all, you need to become the customer. Buy from as many sellers (both on and off eBay) as you can reasonably afford. Make notes of your experience and identify the best parts of the customer experience from each while also remaining conscious of the negative aspects of the experience that you will avoid in your own business. Find your niche in the category and provide a customer experience unlike any other.

Chapter 21
Sourcing products to sell

Finding the right product to sell in Australia's busiest marketplace is one of the most important things you will need to do. To identify the 'right product', here are some of the crucial things you need to consider:

- Can I find a supplier who has the right to sell it to me for resale on eBay?

- Can I find more than one supplier in case something goes wrong with my initial supplier relationship?

- Can I rely on enough supply?

- Can I store (warehouse) the product properly or is there an opportunity to have others store it for me?

- Can I purchase it at a price that will give me a clear profit?

- Is it already for sale on eBay? If yes, can I compete with the average selling price and will that give me clear profit? If no, why is no-one else selling it? How easy would it be for another seller to source the same product and sell more profitably than I can?

- Do I know enough about the product to answer all of my buyers' questions?

- Can I send the product throughout Australia easily? If I need to expand into overseas markets, can I send internationally without exorbitant postage or export/import costs?

- Is it a fragile product or will it withstand delivery easily?

- Would I be breaking any laws or any eBay policies by selling the product?

- Is it the kind of product that buyers might want to return—for example, is it susceptible to performance issues or flaws that will increase my operating costs? That is, can I afford to refund or exchange a percentage of my sales and still maintain my profit?

- Is it the kind of product that will need professional installation and/ or ongoing customer support? Do I need to consider warranties or a guarantee?

- Is the product subject to any limits on resale, such as exclusivity rights or brand ownership? (Refer to chapter 33 for more information on the Verified Rights Owner (VeRO) program.)

Once you've considered all of these questions, you can begin looking for the right product a little more seriously. The one question I've been asked most often over my years of helping eBay sellers is 'What should I sell?', and this question is asked by the smallest right up to the very largest eBay seller! If only the answer was as straightforward as people seem to think it should be, or there was some magical equation we could apply to eBay data to generate a list of results. In short, however, there is no magic answer and you have just as much chance of choosing the right (or the wrong) product to sell as the next business.

Following are some options you may wish to consider for sourcing the right products to sell on eBay, but remember to consider carefully the 'right product' questions outlined earlier in this chapter, and the profit considerations outlined in chapter 22.

Use your network

Take a moment to think of every close friend and family member you have and make a list of the companies or industries they work for. I did this myself before arriving at the answer that had been staring me in the face for the first eight years I'd been working at eBay: I could leverage my dad's contacts in the industry he'd been a part of for more than 30 years. It wasn't until I created my network list that I could clearly see the opportunities.

After you've developed your network list, narrow down your options using the product questions and profit equations in this book. Then take your select few network connections out for lunch or a coffee and ask them about their industry and whether it would be possible for you, through mutual connections, to source products to resell.

When it comes to the crunch, you may have to present a business plan to convince the manufacturer or supplier that having an eBay business sell their products is right for the future of their business. The same applies for approaching a business by cold calling (that is, contacting someone you do not know, usually by phone).

It might sound obvious, but don't forget to include the company you work for, if you're employed by one that manufactures, wholesales or resells products.

Cold calling

Think of the products you're most passionate about, and the ones that satisfy all of the questions you asked earlier in this chapter. Complete your research to ascertain what kind of opportunity there is for selling those products on eBay and create a simple business case for each. The current slump in retail (and this extends to manufacturers and wholesalers of retail products) makes this an ideal time to approach companies to suggest eBay as a fast, convenient and successful channel for expanding existing business and customer bases.

A successful business case should include the following:

* *Evidence of your understanding of the current status of the market for the product (in general) and the company behind it.* You will need to conduct internet research or utilise your network to get the right information here; for example, look for annual reports, retail sales reports and industry trend reports.

* *A brief analysis of the current situation for the product on eBay.* This includes popularity, sales, selling prices, existing sellers, gaps in the market, and marketing opportunities.

* *A brief overview of the new eBay and why it's a sensible complementary channel for existing businesses.* Use the knowledge you've gained from reading this book and internet research to create five to 10 newsworthy bullet points.

* *A brief background on you and your career.* Why are you the right person to be reselling this business's products, and why are you the right person to resell on eBay? Outline your eBay knowledge and experience.

* *An outline of how your business will be structured.* Where it will be based, how products will be stored, packaged and shipped, insurance considerations, how customer service will be provided, what level of reporting will be available (see part V).

- *A forecast for annual sales on eBay and anticipated sales prices.* Use your knowledge from the research you conduct in chapter 22.

- *A guide to how you want the relationship with the company to operate.* Will it be goods on consignment (you pay only for what you sell on eBay), sales price less discount, or set purchase price? Outline minimum order quantities, any exclusivity agreements and access to intellectual property, such as catalogue information, logos and product images.

All of the above should be presented in either a printed portfolio or as an electronic presentation such as PowerPoint. You can find ready-made templates by conducting an internet search. Make sure you present a professional, polished and accurate business case, and be sure to present it to the correct decision maker within the company (there's no point wasting an hour of the receptionist's time if it is the sales director who would make the final decision). Be prepared to spend some time on this part of the process; multiple meetings may be required before an agreement is met. Other companies may be so impressed by your knowledge and proposal that things happen much faster than expected, so approach the business only once you have the necessary operations in place to get started straight away.

Buy products in bulk for resale

There are countless websites you could consider for sourcing your products in bulk so you can break them down into individual or smaller sizes and resell on eBay. Finding a website that no other seller has discovered is part of the trick to making this a successful product sourcing strategy. Of course, you could scour international eBay sites or use the Asian wholesale website Alibaba (www.alibaba.com), but scores of other Australian eBay sellers are doing the same thing, so the chances of your finding something unique and profitable may be quite slim. You can work on a smaller scale by searching eBay for poorly described, poorly photographed or misspelled products that are unlikely to attract much buyer interest—by purchasing and 're-presenting' them to eBay customers you may be able to realise a profit. Although this will be hit-and-miss, and unscalable, if you find a few hidden gems it can be well worth your time.

You can find greater success by approaching a company that is not yet online, or perhaps one that does not yet have a presence in the Australian market at all. You will need to present a convincing business case, as outlined earlier in the chapter, but persevering through an arduous search to find the right company can be rewarding. Some of eBay's largest and most profitable sellers source direct from the manufacturer in Asia, and having an exclusivity agreement will help secure an even more prosperous future.

Another opportunity exists in sourcing bulk supply of products from bricks-and-mortar retail or perhaps from a wholesale outlet. A great source can also be physical auction houses that regularly sell seized or liquidated businesses' products at a fraction of the market value. This can be especially rewarding if you source the last supply of a particular product line, but less successful if you buy products already widely available at the discounted price. One of the challenges of this approach is that it is much harder to secure guaranteed lines of supply and to establish consistency in a given category.

Make products to sell

Many artisans, artists, craft enthusiasts and other creative types use eBay to sell the products they have created with their own hands. If you have the time and resources to create a steady supply of products and sell at a profit, this can be a successful way to operate. One thing to bear in mind here is the time it takes to turn your raw materials into finished products; businesses often forget to calculate production time as a specific cost (we'll return to this in the next chapter).

Scavenge

This might seem like an odd suggestion, but over the years I have met a considerable number of people who scavenge for discarded products to resell on eBay. Although they will only interest buyers in the second-hand market, if you find the right products you will undoubtedly attract buyer interest. The other great thing about this method of sourcing is that aside from transport to collect it, and time spent restoring or repairing it, you have virtually no upfront costs, so your chances of making a profit are greatly increased. It can be hard and dirty work finding the right products to sell and it's difficult to scale a business based on one-off and unique finds, but it can be done if you have a natural flair for finding in-demand rarities or have a gift for restoration.

Product expansion

Wherever you find your products to sell on eBay, my advice is: never stop looking for more. It's impossible to predict buyer trends (what's hot one day might be impossible to sell the next), competitive threats (a bigger seller might come in to compete against you and be able to sell at a much lower price), supplier changes (changes in their resale policies or bankruptcy, for example) and a host of other factors that may impact on your ability to sell your chosen product. A sensible business owner is constantly on the lookout for more, better products and for opportunities to expand. Even if you have a successful future selling one product, why not consider selling more if you can grow your profits by doing so?

Always carry your eBay business card around with you (it's very cheap to get these produced by a professional printer) and ensure it includes the URL (website address) to find your eBay products or store (for more information, see chapter 23), and a list of the brands or products you sell. You never know when someone at your next family function or business event, or on a train — anyone, anywhere — might be able to connect you with your next line of profitable products. Consider attending as many expos and product conferences as you reasonably can and take every opportunity to expand your network.

Chapter 22
Budgeting for profit

I once met an eBay seller who told me he could not afford to pay his eBay fees because his profit margin was only 3 per cent. I asked him if he'd visited his business model and assessed ways of reducing his postage costs, electricity bill, transport costs or the time spent packing products to find other ways to increase his profit margin. It wasn't a trick question. I was trying to help him understand that eBay fees are one small part of an eBay business's profit equation. Many of the costs that go into running an eBay business are within your control, while others simply are not. To be a successful eBay business you need to be zealous in reducing those costs within your control. You could argue as much time should be spent reducing costs as dealing with your customers and products.

It may seem odd to include a profit calculator *before* we've covered off all the costs involved in selling on eBay. But you need to appreciate your profit margin before you purchase products and begin selling them on eBay, so it's prudent to ensure you fully understand the eBay profit equation before going any further into advanced selling techniques.

Let's start with some very basic definitions and equations:

Gross sales (or gross profit or income) is the total amount of goods sold by your business plus any additional income (100 shirts sold at $30 each = $3000 gross sales).

Cost of sales is every expense you incur in the course of making a sale. This includes: purchasing products, marketing costs, and labour and running costs. For this example, let's say our cost of sales for the 100 shirts is $2000. We'll cover this in more detail in a moment.

Net profit is gross sales minus the cost of sales. As an equation, your net profit looks like:

Gross profit − Cost of sales = Net profit

For this specific example, our equation is:

$3000 − $2000 = $1000 net profit

The final component is to work out your profit as a percentage, or your profit margin. As an equation it looks like:

$$\frac{Net\ profit}{Gross\ profit} = Profit\ margin$$

For this specific example, our equation is:

$$\frac{\$1000}{\$3000} = 33\%\ profit\ margin$$

Now we've covered the basics, let's put it into a practical example using a typical eBay business model. In the 2012–13 financial year, a particular seller we'll call 'Groovy Duds' sold $105 000 worth of clothing on eBay (inclusive of GST). To tally her total gross sales she includes any additional income, which in her case comprises $23 000 in money collected from buyers for postage. (While she sells some items with free postage, more expensive items attract a registered post charge and other buyers elect to pay for express or courier options.) Her total income for the financial year therefore is $128 000.

It's imperative for Groovy Duds to now calculate all of the costs incurred in making the $128 000. For the typical eBay business, things to consider would be:

- the cost of purchasing the shirts (including purchase price, shipping costs, and travel to and from the supplier)
- all eBay fees (insertion, feature, final value, subscription)
- PayPal or Paymate fees
- credit card processing fees (if applicable)
- actual postage costs
- packaging costs (packing tape, bubble wrap, envelopes, boxes, satchels and so on)
- business insurance
- fuel costs in taking packages to the post office every day
- electricity costs (for running her computer, overhead lighting, printer and so on)
- phone calls made to buyers
- printing costs (paper, printer cartridges)

- stationery (return address stickers, thank you notes, business cards and so on)

- internet connection costs

- the cost of using office or warehouse space (if she operates out of her home she should calculate the percentage of her rent or mortgage dedicated to running her eBay business)

- accountant and lawyer fees (associated specifically with the running of the business)

- software costs (if she's purchased any software specific to running her business, such as MYOB or Excel)

- the cost of refunds, lost or damaged products, exchanges or processing returns

- staff costs (staff who process orders, deal with customers, package products. If you're a sole operator, do you pay yourself an income? Even if you don't, you should calculate for yourself an hourly rate of costs. After all, if your net profit before this calculation is $300 per month and it takes you 300 hours per month to run your eBay business, you're paying yourself the equivalent of the grand sum of $1 an hour, so you'd have to question whether the business is viable.)

- GST and tax payments, and income considerations

- any other costs (such as wear and tear on equipment, furniture, storage solutions, attendance at seminars or training courses).

It's a sensible idea to keep a monthly account of each of these costs and your sales so you can continually monitor your operating margins. You can do this using either a software program such as Excel or a simple printed spreadsheet. More advanced business accounting software such as MYOB is also available. When your margin falls below your set reasonable level, you need to increase sales or lower costs, or both, to improve your business's bottom line (net profit).

Only when you've accurately calculated all these costs can you truly begin to assess whether your eBay business is profitable — that is, providing you with a reasonable net profit. There's no set guide as to what is reasonable. A 5 per cent profit margin on a $1 million business gives you $50 000 net profit per year; 15 per cent on a $25 000 business gives you only $3750 net profit. Only you can decide what is reasonable for your needs, but read back over the extensive list of costs earlier in this chapter. What could you be doing to lower your annual cost for each one? Negotiating, looking for alternative suppliers or providers, agreeing to longer term contracts, or forming a cooperative with friends or other businesses are just a few simple avenues to cost reductions.

If you have an existing business and are now expanding onto eBay, be sure to include all of the associated costs from your existing business in your eBay channel's profitability assessment. It's tempting to assume your eBay sales come at no additional cost, but the most reliable way to assess eBay business profitability is to accurately measure the cost per product.

One of the largest and most costly investments of any business, however, is time. In the following chapters we'll look at ways to streamline your eBay business, saving you time and effort. Efficiency is often the key to profitability.

Chapter 23

Setting up your business operations

Before you begin selling on eBay, take the time to set up your business for future success. While some of these operations may not seem important now, you may regret not having established them prior to getting busy selling your products and dealing with your customers. Even if you have an existing business outside of eBay, some of these steps should still be completed now.

Register as an eBay business

In chapter 1 we completed registration together. You'll notice we included the option to register as an eBay business. One of the main advantages of this is that you are able to add your business name to your account, which means correspondence from you to your customers appears more professional and your invoices from eBay will be addressed to your business name, making it easier for tax calculations. In some eBay markets, registration as a business is mandatory if your sales turnover exceeds a set amount. While this is not yet the case in Australia, it's something to bear in mind for the future.

If you have already registered as a seller on eBay and want to convert your account to business, this can be done by clicking My eBay at the top of any eBay page. Hover your mouse over the *Account* tab then click Personal information (if you are registered as a business it will appear as Business information). Click Edit next to the information you want to change.

Register as a PayPal/ Paymate business

If you haven't registered as a business account on PayPal or Paymate (if you'll be accepting these payment options), it's important to do so now. Business accounts receive preferential fee rates (as low as 1.1 per cent on

PayPal compared with the 2.4 per cent starting fee). We'll cover more on fees and payment processing later in chapter 28. On PayPal there is also the bonus of multi-user access (your staff now or in the future can access specific features of PayPal as stipulated by you, rather than accessing everything by using your password).

Note that registering as a business on PayPal or Paymate may require you to provide more evidence of business ownership or identification (such as a driver's licence or business name documentation), but the process is fast and usually hassle-free. For more information on PayPal (www.paypal.com.au), click the *Business* tab at the top of the page and for Paymate (www.paymate.com), hover your mouse over the Sellers link.

Register your business name

If you have a business outside of eBay, it's likely you've already registered your business name. You may wish to consider registering a new business identity for the eBay component of your business that is aligned with your current name. This will help keep your eBay sales separate from your existing business.

For those without an existing business, it may be a good idea to register your business name before you decide on your eBay brand. This is a measure for future growth: if your business name is already taken you could run into problems in the future with trying to maintain your branding on and off eBay.

First you will need an Australian Business Number (ABN) so your business can be identified. You can apply for an ABN online at www.abr.gov.au. Once you have an ABN, you can then register a business name with the Australian Securities and Investments Commission (ASIC) website at www.asic.gov.au. Both processes take 15 to 20 minutes to complete and attract a fee.

Register a bank account

Once you have the necessary documentation, you should also open a bank account in your business's name. This is the bank account you should link to your PayPal or Paymate accounts so that funds received from buyers can be placed into this account for your access. If you choose to accept bank deposits from buyers, this will also ensure you have consistent branding.

Register a URL

Similarly, while you may have no immediate intention of starting your own website outside of eBay, in the future you may wish to expand your operations and sell direct to online shoppers. Many large eBay sellers do this to complement their eBay businesses. It's a good idea to register your website address today so you will always have it in the future. You can conduct an internet search to find websites where you can purchase domain names (website addresses); depending on your future plans you may wish to register for .com.au (Australian) as well as .com (American) addresses. Different providers charge different fees but you can expect to pay an annual ownership fee for every domain name you register.

To summarise, you should have a consistent business name across your eBay user ID, your PayPal account, your ABN, your ASIC-registered business name, an off-eBay website and a bank account. Now you have all of the names and accounts properly registered, you need to think about the smooth physical running of your eBay business.

Organise your office layout

If you're operating your eBay business from home, it's important to have a dedicated area, free from distractions, for a computer, printer and storage of any documentation and other materials you may need to run your business. I've seen home-run offices where sellers operate from their bedrooms, but it's not practical or sustainable over the longer term. If operating from home, my best advice is to dedicate one room to your eBay business that may also include space for storing the products you intend to sell.

Look online for information regarding ergonomics (healthy office design and furnishing) to ensure you are protecting your health and wellbeing. What may begin as 30 minutes' work per day could easily escalate to three hours: so if you don't have the right desk, chair and keyboard, for example, you could be causing yourself longer term harm. Keep your computer close to your products and a printer. You don't want to be running from one end of the house to the other, or from your house to your shed, every time you need to match an order on your screen to your physical products. While this might be a handy way of keeping fit, remember that we're in the business of profit, and any time wasted eats into your profit margin.

It's a good idea to install a few key software programs on your computer. The ones I use most in operating my eBay business are Excel and Word (or the Macintosh equivalents, Numbers and Pages). I use Excel to track my monthly sales and it's also the format that most eBay reports will be read in. I use Word to create my item descriptions, place orders with my suppliers and cut-and-paste answers to most commonly asked questions.

If you have an existing business, I advise you to set up a separate area for your eBay operations. You will more than likely need to dedicate at least one person to your eBay business so you should dedicate at least one computer to it. Some larger retailers have fallen into the trap of assuming that an existing staff member will be able to squeeze running an eBay business into their day job, but they have quickly realised that a dedicated team member is the most efficient way of operating. Dedicating at least one computer to eBay will mean that staff can check eBay at any given time and all related information can be stored on the same device.

For existing businesses, consider also your staff's core competencies. Retail floor staff may not have the suitable experience to deal with online customers, or to pick, pack and ship your products most efficiently. Your eBay business should be run by someone with key computer skills, online selling experience, and the ability to pack the products and oversee logistics with high efficiency. Paying retail floor staff an hourly wage to perform these functions efficiently might cost more than the wage you would pay a warehouse employee, for example.

In my experience, it's easier and more ergonomically effective to run your eBay business from a desktop or laptop than it is using a tablet or mobile phone. While iPad and iPhone apps can be helpful in identifying when a sale has occurred, the relatively small screen sizes make frequent order processing laborious.

Organise your warehouse layout

Only the largest eBays sellers operate out of a warehouse, or perhaps you are an existing business that already operates from one. In using the term *warehouse*, I refer broadly to the place where your products are stored. For some people it's in their house, their garage or a storage facility, while for others a fully automated warehouse might be used. However you're set up, it's imperative that your products are accurately ordered so you or your staff can access them as quickly as possible. Wasted time eats into your profit margin.

Depending on the number of products you keep in stock at any one time, it may even be worth speaking to a logistics professional to ensure you are operating as efficiently as possible and in line with standard occupational health and safety practices. I've seen eBay sellers with boxes strewn all over the house, and warehouses where products are placed in the order they are received, which has little relevance to the order in which they will need to be picked.

Consider some of the following systems:

- *Alphabetisation*. Use product names to store them alphabetically. Ensure a standard method of naming is used — for example, brand, make or model, rather than a combination of all three.

- *Product code*. Most products come with a manufacturer code or barcode. You could consider storing them in numerical order.

- *Storage labelling*. Clearly label your storage areas. Having products in order doesn't help if there is no signage to differentiate between various areas or shelves.

- *Storage map*. Consider creating a storage map, and keep this on your computer so you can refer to it if your storage area becomes disordered.

- *Listing notes*. Make notes in your eBay listings that only you and your staff can see, clearly identifying where the product is stored (we'll cover this later in part IV).

- *Storing heavy items*. Keep heavy objects where they are easy to lift. Never place them above head height unless you have the correct equipment to lift them.

- *Separate fragile items*. Keep fragile products in designated areas so you and your staff remember to treat them with care.

- *Lighting and access*. Ensure you can always see your products, labelling and signage clearly and nothing obstructs access to stock. To optimise profit you need to be able to get to any individual product as quickly as possible.

If you're an existing retailer, my advice is to keep your eBay (or online) products apart from your retail store products. It's a simple profit equation: by storing them in your retail store you are paying expensive retail rent and other overheads on those products. Where possible, storing them in a warehouse (usually less rent paid per product) means you are optimising your profit. Keeping your online and bricks-and-mortar stock separate also means that online customers are less likely to be frustrated in the event that your website or eBay listing claims you have the item in stock but it cannot be found in your retail store. Remember that your online customers are Australia-wide (or global) and they shop 24 hours per day, seven days per week, so you have the potential for much greater buyer demand than those who happen to enter your shop during retail opening hours.

Speak to your accountant/ tax adviser

If you've done your research correctly, you should be able to forecast what your initial eBay sales will be. Businesses that turn over more than $75 000 per year need to be registered for GST, and the Australian Taxation Office (ATO) regularly conducts audits of eBay sellers to check against tax returns. eBay is legally bound to supply the ATO with this information. If it's more than a hobby—that is, if you're sourcing products with the intent to resell on eBay—you should consider what the tax and GST implications might be. It's a good idea to consult an accountant or a tax adviser at the outset to ensure you are properly registered, are collecting the correct information and have considered all of the tax benefits that you may be entitled to (as well as the payments you may need to make).

Chapter 24
Your eBay brand

Earlier in part IV I mentioned the four Ps of retail. The fourth one is *promotion*. On eBay, promotion takes various forms, beginning with your eBay brand.

Brand consistency

It's vitally important that everything you do on eBay is presented with a consistent, memorable brand. Your brand should be clearly identifiable in the following items:

- *Your eBay user ID*. Choose an ID that is associated with the kinds of products you sell. If you started on eBay with a personal ID that could not be considered a business brand, change your ID before you begin selling as a business. If you have an existing business name outside of eBay, it may already be taken as an eBay user ID (user names are global). If this is the case, try an extension at the end of your business name, such as abcgardens_australia or abcgardens_online, to make your eBay ID unique.

- *Your eBay store name and design*. There is more information on this later, in chapter 27.

- *Your listing title*. The words you choose should include your brand and a tone that is consistent with your brand's personality. Words like 'bargain' are okay if that's the image you want to present, but phrases outlining services such as '90-day returns' and '3-year warranty' suggest a more professional operation.

- *Your item descriptions*. Clear and consistent branding and design should reflect your brand image.

- *Your email address*.

- *Your PayPal and/or Paymate address*.

- *Your bank account*. This is important if you choose to accept bank deposit from buyers.

- *The feedback you leave for others.* 'Thank you for buying from [insert your business name here]' is professional and memorable.

- *Your packaging.* There is more information on this later, in chapter 31.

- *Stationery.* This might include thank-you notes and business cards.

- *The tone of your communications with buyers.*

- *The use of your logo in eBay communications.* We'll show you how to do this later in this chapter and in chapter 27.

If you have already registered and want to update any aspect of your eBay information, you can do so by clicking My eBay at the top of any eBay page. Hover your mouse over the *Account* tab then click Personal information (if you are registered as a business it will appear as Business information). Click Edit next to the information you want to change.

Brand relevance

Think carefully about the products you're selling on eBay and the colours and design of your eBay brand. Black might not be the best choice for children's clothing but it works well for auto parts, for example. Any images (other than products) within your branding will also affect your brand's personality. Is clothing modelled by people or draped on mannequins? Are products shown in situ or have you just photographed the box they come in? Are your listings packed with helpful advice for getting the most out of the product? Considering questions such as these will help you define your image more carefully. If you have an existing brand, are you selling all your products on eBay or just excess and clearance stock? If the latter, you might want to consider altering your brand image slightly for eBay so your existing customers can tell the difference between the two.

Avoid using particular words in conjunction with online selling, and specific categories. For example, earlier in the book we used the fictitious user ID 'Groovy Duds'. While duds is an acceptable colloquialism for clothes, the other meaning of *dud* is failure, so it's perhaps not the best branding for online selling, when buyers have never met you and need to pay for products they haven't seen.

You'll find this advice repeated many times throughout this book: carefully check your spelling! Incorrect spelling not only presents an unprofessional image but can also be difficult for buyers to remember. Deliberately incorrect spelling is often overused in business names and may send the wrong message. ('Kool Knits', for example, not only is incorrectly spelt but also implies that the knitted products are cool, rather than warm.)

Make your brand name and brand design memorable. There are millions of eBay sellers throughout the world and anything you can do to stand out from the crowd by creating something buyers relate to will help ensure repeat visits, and repeat sales.

A professional design

Professionally branded eBay sellers really do stand out on the site. Professionalism instils buyer confidence and sets you apart from your competitors. After all, if two identical items are for sale at the same price but from two different sellers, what is going to convince a buyer to purchase from you?

Marketing and brand design agencies can help you create a unique brand name, image and design, although this service will usually come at a considerable price. You can also download logo-designing software or use a logo design website to create something that looks more professional than you might otherwise be able to produce on your own.

Another idea is to contact your local TAFE or design school and ask students to design your logo and branding for a much smaller fee than you'd expect to pay an established agency. Some students may even be willing to do this for free if they can add the design to their portfolio.

An internet search will also reveal companies dedicated to eBay business design, with prices ranging from a few hundred to a few thousand dollars. While this kind of investment may seem high, think back to the research you conducted for your products. Did some sellers look more professional than others, and how did their sales compare with the less professional looking sellers? Some eBay businesses I've spoken with have seen a spike in sales once they've had their brand professionally designed, though of course there is no guarantee this will happen.

Having your brand professionally designed will also make it more transferable across eBay, your own website, your stationery and everywhere else your brand will be seen.

Chapter 25

Listing your products and managing inventory

In part III we covered basic selling procedures, including listing your products for sale. As you will have noticed, this was a fairly manual process and not scalable for listing large volumes of product. Some of eBay's larger sellers list thousands, even millions, of products on the sites, and there are ways to do this more efficiently than by entering every single product into the Sell your item form, as covered in part III. Let's begin with the information you should include within your listing.

Create a professional listing

When you're operating a professional eBay business, your product listings need to be the equivalent of a high-end retail catalogue. Polished, well-designed and comprehensive listings instil buyer confidence and help you secure initial, and repeat, sales. As well as completing every section of eBay's selling form template (such as item specifics and returns), here are a few non-negotiable inclusions for serious business sellers.

Photography must be of the highest standard, with clean, crisp images and natural lighting, like something you would see in a retail catalogue. Upload large photos (a minimum of 1600 pixels per side) so buyers can enlarge them to see finer detail. Include multiple photos to show different angles, styles and close-up details (such as colour and material patterns).

Comprehensive product information, with every conceivable piece of information about the product, should be included. Consider adding not only the brand, model, model number, size, colour, weight, dimensions, materials, manufacture details, contents and specifications, but also instructions for correct use or installation, information about optimal operation and suggestions for use (where applicable).

In your listing description, include information about your payment, shipping and returns policies, but don't overwhelm buyers with too many details, terms or conditions, and don't use language that is threatening or aggressive. If in doubt, refer to your favourite retailer and emulate the language and tone they use.

Always accept returns and specify a 'no questions asked' policy. Consider using a reply paid service via your post office so buyers don't have to pay for return postage, and consider adding a warranty or guarantee for further peace of mind.

Create links within your listing to your other products for sale on eBay or in your eBay store. Where possible, choose to highlight complementary products to encourage multiple purchases from the same buyer. eBay includes some 'add links' functionality within its Standard selling form, but a basic knowledge of HTML is all you need to insert links.

Wherever possible, give buyers an indication of recommended retail price (but only where you can substantiate this with proof) and highlight the saving they are making by purchasing from you.

Inform your buyers of the type of packaging you use to further instil confidence, particularly if you're sending fragile or expensive products.

Use one font consistently throughout your listing, and make sure it's not too wide for standard computer screens (check your listings using multiple internet programs and on a variety of computers). Don't use watermarks or graffiti (superimposing writing over the top of the image) on your product photographs—not only do they look unprofessional but they may soon be banned by eBay.

Triple-check your spelling, and have someone else check it for you too. There are no excuses for incorrect spelling if you're running a professional business.

Choose your item title keywords very carefully. Do not use overly expressive or flowery language — stick to core product or service offerings. Adding vaguely associated keywords may have a negative impact on your standing in Best match. Stick to the simple basics: condition, brand, creator, quantity, size/dimensions, colour, material, style, model, weight and so on.

Consider using a subtitle to further highlight your customer service offerings, such as 100-day returns, free postage to anywhere in Australia or tracked shipping. Always add item specifics in the listing flow—these not only add relevance within Best match but are also how some buyers help refine their searches. Add your own item specifics if eBay's provided list is not extensive enough.

If your product is covered in eBay's catalogue, always incorporate the catalogue information in your listing—it adds more detailed product specifications and a more professional feel to your description.

In short, if your listing doesn't look as though it's directly from one of Australia's best retail websites, you're wasting an opportunity to drive more sales and improve your profitability. You are, in effect, enticing buyers into your store to purchase, and the more appealing you can make that experience, the more you will encourage traffic to your listings and increase sales via checkout.

Now let's take a look at ways to save time in uploading your high-quality listings to eBay.

Excel and concatenate

You can save time and effort by using a straightforward function within Excel called *concatenate* to complete your listing descriptions (the same functionality is available in Macintosh Numbers). You'll still have to manually enter information such as category and price into the selling form, but a lot of this can be cut-and-pasted from your Excel template. Most computers come with Excel, but you can also download it for Windows and Mac computers via the Microsoft website at www.microsoftstore.com for around $200. Using this system in the past I have reduced the time spent on eBay's Standard selling form from around ten minutes per product to around two minutes. For 200 products you can easily save yourself 20 hours' work.

Following is an example of how to complete listings quickly. Write your first listing within eBay's Sell your item form and capture the following information:

- *Title*—Yates Seeds Tomato Roma 0.2g Brand New Australian Free Postage

- *Item specifics*—capture any information written in the free-form fields, not chosen from a drop-down such as Tomato; Roma.

- *Item description* — copy all of the information you entered, such as:

Tomato — Roma

Deep red, pear-shaped fruit. Ideal for salads, bottling, soups and sauces. The perfect tomato for sun-drying.

Key features

Medium fruit, ideal in containers, doesn't need staking.

Browse the entire Yates Gardening range. Be sure to add Yates Gardening to your favourite eBay seller list!

Postage and handling

Postage is FREE on all orders. All our seeds are packed by plant-loving professionals and we dispatch within two days of receiving payment. Sorry but we cannot send to countries outside Australia.

Payment

We prefer PayPal but also accept bank deposit. Please ensure you label your payment clearly with your eBay user ID to ensure speedy delivery.

Planting position

Full sun.

Sowing instructions

Sow direct in warm conditions or raise in trays of Yates Seed Raising Mix. Firm down and keep moist. Transplant when 5–7 cm high.

- *Price* — $3.50
- *Quantity* — 50

We will assume that the postage, payment, returns and other information is standard across all of our listings.

First, open a blank Excel spreadsheet. Next, label your first column as Title 1. Copy all generic information (that will apply to all your titles) before the product-specific information and break each component out into separate columns. In this example:

	Column A	Column B	Column C	Column D
Row 1	Yates	Tomato Roma	0.2g	Brand New Australian Free Postage

Now, moving down each row, copy each piece of generic information, and enter the product-specific information, as in this example:

	Column A	Column B	Column C	Column D
Row 1	Yates	Tomato Roma	0.2g	Brand New Australian Free Postage
Row 2	Yates	Tomato Cherry	0.5g	Brand New Australian Free Postage
Row 3	Yates	Tomato Heirloom	0.3g	Brand New Australian Free Postage

Finally, in column E1, you need to enter the concatenate formula. Concatenate turns text in a series of cells into one stream of text or a sentence. Enter the formula:

=Concatenate (A1,B1,C1,D1)

and copy the formula into cells E2, E3 and so on, as below:

	Column A	Column B	Column C	Column D	Column E
Row 1	Yates	Tomato Roma	0.2g	Brand New Australian Free Postage	=Concatenate (A1,B1,C1,D1)
Row 2	Yates	Tomato Cherry	0.5g	Brand New Australian Free Postage	=Concatenate (A2,B2,C2,D2)
Row 3	Yates	Tomato Heirloom	0.3g	Brand New Australian Free Postage	=Concatenate (A3,B3,C3,D3)

Now you will be able to copy cell E1 and paste it into the title field in the Sell your item form on eBay, and do the same for each new listing. In columns F and G you can list item specifics (*Tomato, Roma* and so on) and in columns H and I you can list price and quantity.

Now we get to item description, which is a bit more complicated. You need to know two basic HTML codes to help eBay read your description from Excel and keep consistent formatting. <H1> must be used every time you create a new heading, and to finish the heading you need to enter </H1>; <p> needs to be used every time you start a new paragraph. So, following this principle, enter as per the example below, continuing until the entire product description has been completed in the columns:

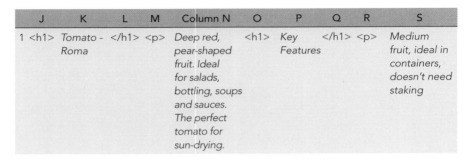

J	K	L	M	Column N	O	P	Q	R	S
1 <h1>	Tomato - Roma	</h1>	<p>	Deep red, pear-shaped fruit. Ideal for salads, bottling, soups and sauces. The perfect tomato for sun-drying.	<h1>	Key Features	</h1>	<p>	Medium fruit, ideal in containers, doesn't need staking

Then in each row copy the generic information and enter the product-specific information just as you did for the title fields above. Finally, enter the concatenate formula in the last column, being sure to include all the cells from J1 right up until your next-to-last column so you capture all of the information in your Excel description. You'll now be able to copy and paste from your last column into the description area within the Sell your item form. Remember to paste your Excel information into the *HTML* tab of the description field so eBay can read your HTML code.

This Excel spreadsheet can then be used as your product inventory and updated with monthly sales so you can keep track of how much stock you have remaining and which products need to be reordered from your suppliers.

It might sound like a lot of time to set this up, but my experience using concatenate saved me a considerable amount of time previously spent copying and pasting from a Word document. Have a go in Excel first and see if you think this is a good way to save time for your level of computer skills. If not, there are other options!

Optimise your time with Selling Manager Pro

eBay has an inventory management tool known as Selling Manager. The basic version is free to use but the more advanced version (Selling Manager Pro) is $9.95 per month, or free if you subscribe to an eBay store. Pro is recommended for businesses, as it contains more automation to help you optimise your time and therefore your profit. To subscribe (you can unsubscribe at any time), click Customer support at the top of any eBay page, type 'Selling Manager' into the help search field and click *Search*. On the right, click Using Selling Manager and Selling Manager Pro. The tool has many functions but let's begin by creating a listing.

First, click Sell at the top of any eBay page then, beneath the category suggester, click Create templates (see figure 25.1). Alternatively, click Manage templates to edit an existing template, duplicate an existing template or create a new one.

Figure 25.1: creating a Selling Manager template

Next, complete the rest of your product information as covered in part III. However, in the Sell your item form, consider two more advanced options beneath the categories section (see figure 25.2, overleaf). Under 'Save to inventory' click Add product details or Edit product details if you're using an existing product template—this will create a new product for your inventory management system. As the name suggests, a new product should be created for each addition to your inventory. A number of different templates can be added for each product (for example, a Buy it now template, an auction template, a template where free postage is offered or a template where postage is charged). Fill in the product details in the pop-up that appears, then click *Save*.

Figure 25.2: creating inventory and multiple variations

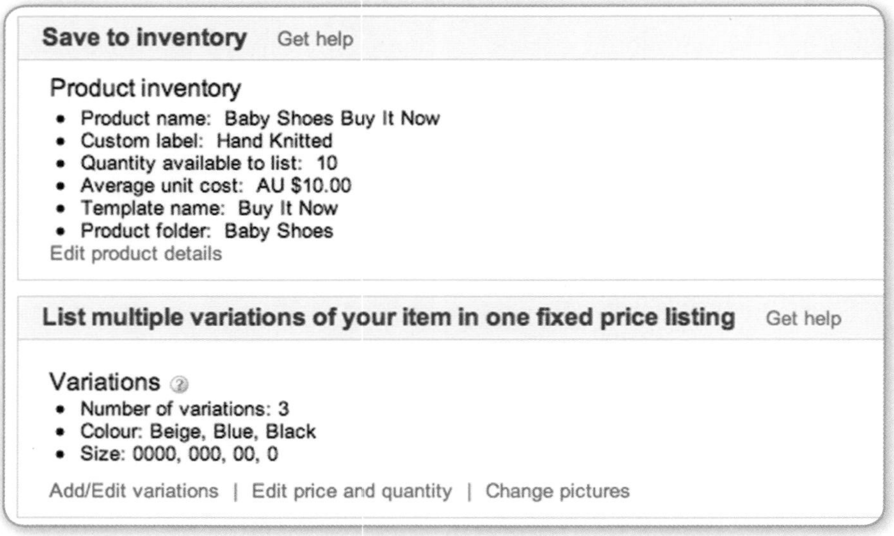

Save to inventory   Get help

Product inventory
- Product name: Baby Shoes Buy It Now
- Custom label: Hand Knitted
- Quantity available to list: 10
- Average unit cost: AU $10.00
- Template name: Buy It Now
- Product folder: Baby Shoes

Edit product details

List multiple variations of your item in one fixed price listing   Get help

Variations ⓘ
- Number of variations: 3
- Colour: Beige, Blue, Black
- Size: 0000, 000, 00, 0

Add/Edit variations | Edit price and quantity | Change pictures

To save time and (in some instances) listing fees, click *Create variations* (or <u>Add/Edit variations</u> if you have already created some) if your product is one of a series of similar products. For example, if you are selling multiple sizes or colours of the one product, or perhaps left-handed and right-handed versions of the same product, you can list both products within the one listing and buyers can make their choice from the View item page. Fill in the relevant variations then click *Continue*. Next, add the SKUs or variation combinations you have available for purchase (such as pink size 0 or pink size 00) and click *Continue*. Now add multiple photos to show the range of different product types available within this listing. Finally, add price and the quantity available and click *Save*. Having multiple variations within one listing will also help boost the number of sales per listing for this product, and this, in turn, contributes to your receiving a higher position in the Best match algorithm (more information on this later in part IV).

Creating more buyer interest

If you list more than 10 items within a single listing, my advice is to hide from buyers the actual number available. If you show that you have 300 in stock, you will reduce any sense of urgency in the buyer

Complete the rest of the Sell your item form as outlined in part III. On the last page of the Sell your item form you have the option to *Submit & Save Listing* (sends your listing live to eBay and also saves the template in your Selling Manager inventory) or Save template for later (saves the template in the Sell your item form for you to complete at a later date).

Now that we have created one product with one template, it's fast and easy to duplicate this for all our other products. First we need to access our inventory within Selling Manager. This can be done by clicking My eBay at the top of any eBay page then Selling manager pro then Inventory (see figure 25.3).

Figure 25.3: managing inventory in Selling Manager Pro

In this example we have created a new product for 'Tomato Grosse Lisse' and saved it to a new folder called 'New Inventory'. Let's take a closer look at the functionality of the inventory page.

At the top of the page, next to the word 'Folder', choose from a drop-down list any of the folders you have created. Click Manage folders to add new, or delete existing, folders at any time. Next to 'Search Inventory' you can choose from product name, custom label, item title or item ID to search for keywords you enter into the search field. You can also narrow your inventory search by store category (more on this later in part IV) or status (low stock or out of stock). Click **Search** to find matching inventory.

Beneath this is a list of products in our inventory. Click any of the links at the top right of this section to:

- <u>Show all</u>—shows all listings in your product inventory

- <u>Show variations</u>—shows you the variations you have entered if you completed the multiple variations step in the Sell your item form for this category

- <u>Hide templates</u>—removes from view the templates from each product name

- <u>Customise</u>—changes the information that appears on the inventory page, or the order of results.

Your product appears next. Click on the product name to access more information about it, including its name, the folder it is saved to, its SKU (if you have one to add), average unit cost, average selling price, units sold, quantity unsold, success ratio, quantity available to list and other information. From here you can also click on the link to the template to edit the Sell your item form associated with this product.

You can check the box next to the product name to:

- *Assign automation rules*—allows you to apply any one of a number of automatic listing rules, including:

  - *List according to my schedule*—if you have utilised the schedule listing function in the Sell your item form

  - *Relist once if an item does not sell*—automatically sends your listing live to eBay again if it is not successful the first time

  - *Relist as Fixed Price if an item does not sell*—sends your unsold auction listing live as a fixed price listing if you receive no bids or your auction reserve is not met (or relist your auction at a fixed price)

  - *Relist continually until an item sells*—will keep sending your listing live until you sell at least one product

  - *Relist continually whether it sells or doesn't sell*—keeps relisting your product indefinitely.

- *Remove automation rules*—removes any automated rules you have previously applied to this product

- *Move* — moves the product to a different folder
- *Delete* — removes the product from your inventory
- *Duplicate* — copies this product and edits it with new product information so you do not have to complete a new listing from scratch.

Next to the product listing is a series of columns. From left to right they are:

- *Active* — shows you how many products you have for sale. You can also click on the corresponding number to see live listings.
- *Sold* — shows you how many products you have sold. (You can also click on the corresponding number, for example to see the details of each purchase and link to buyer information.)
- *Unsold* — shows you how many products did not sell successfully
- *Success Ratio* — gives you a percentage of items sold divided by items listed
- *Available to list* — the number of products you have in your warehouse, as stipulated by you during the listing process
- *Last submitted* — the last time you sent that listing live to eBay (does not include automatic relists).

You can click on any of these headings to reorder your inventory by these criteria (lowest to highest or vice versa).

To the right next to the template is a link to Assign automation rules, which was covered earlier in this chapter. You can also click the small arrow next to this to Edit template.

At the bottom right of the listing are several buttons:

- *Sell again* — send your listing live to eBay again
- *Create product* — create a new product (note you can create new products within a listing template)
- *Edit template* — edit this template with updated information
- *Update quantity* — update the quantity available for listing by adding or removing a specified number of products.

Beneath this you will also see a link to upload your inventory. Click on this or File management centre beneath the My eBay navigation on the left of the page to upload an excel file of all of your products. From the file management centre you can also download eBay-friendly templates to ensure your inventory can be uploaded without error. Click <u>Instructions and resources</u> for more information, or <u>Select template</u> to download an example. The information covered in the Excel section of this chapter will help you save time in uploading your inventory via eBay's templates.

Now you have created your inventory, eBay will automatically keep track of your sales success ratio and quantity available, and alert you to products that require reordering. You can take stock of all of your activity by clicking <u>Active</u> in the navigation area on the left. Let's take a closer look at the active listings screen within Selling Manager Pro (see figure 25.4).

Figure 25.4: active listings in Selling Manager Pro

As with the inventory screen, you can search for specific products at the top of the page using any of the four drop-down filters or by clicking on <u>Advanced search</u>. Below this, use the Edit drop-down to edit any individually selected listings or all of your active listings at once. There may be a need to edit all your listings in bulk if, for example, you change your postage options or want to add more information about your services. You can also edit one listing at a time by going to the View item page of any listing and clicking <u>Revise your item</u>. To edit listings in bulk, choose the listings you want to edit by checking the box next to each item title, or choose <u>Edit all [272] listings</u> (the number in brackets will reflect how many listings you have live). This will take you to the Editing screen (see figure 25.5).

Figure 25.5: Selling Manager bulk edit

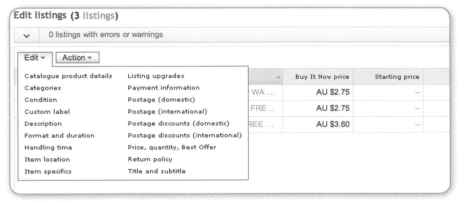

Check the box next to the listings you want to edit, then choose from the editing options in the Edit drop-down. You can edit almost any information within your chosen listings. If you've chosen to edit multiple listings, a pop-up will appear asking whether you want to edit the listings in bulk or individually. Selecting bulk will apply all changes to all chosen listings. You can also use a find-and-replace feature to change your item description; selected text will be replaced with new information as entered by you. Once you have finished making your edits, click *Save and close* then click *Submit all*. The changes will be made instantly to your live listings. Note that some information may not be edited, such as your item title if you have sold products from that listing.

Also on the edit screen, the *Action* button allows you to review the fees associated with the listing, review the changes you have made, remove the listing from the edit screen or cancel the changes you have made. At top right of the screen you can click *Customise* to add or remove columns.

Back on the active listings screen, you can set automation rules for your listings by choosing from the options in the Automation rules drop-down (as covered previously in this chapter). The Action drop-down lets you add or edit a note attached to the listing (for your reference only; a good idea is to outline where the product can be found in your warehouse), end the listing, send live in a different format or save the listing to your Selling Manager inventory.

You can order the columns by the relevant information in each (title, price, available quantity, number of views, item ID, time left), lowest to highest and vice versa, by clicking on the heading. Click <u>Customise</u> at top right to add or remove columns.

In the Actions column to the right, choose from the drop-downs:

- *Send to online auction/fixed price* — relist the listing in a different format

- *Sell similar* — re-creates the listing for you to edit with new information so you do not need to enter all fields over again

- *Revise* — as outlined earlier, revise the listing individually

- *Add to description* — rather than edit your listing, adds a footnote at the bottom of the description for additional information

- *End item* — ends the listing immediately.

Selling Manager Pro also has sales and customer management functionalities that we'll cover later, in chapter 29.

Introducing Turbo Lister

Turbo Lister is eBay's free desktop listing tool available for use on Windows-operated computers.

For more information on Turbo Lister, and to download, click <u>Customer support</u> at the top of any eBay page, enter 'Turbo Lister' in the help search box then click *Search*.

Turbo Lister allows you to easily create, duplicate, upload from Excel and send live to site a large number of listings in a fraction of the time it would take to complete the process manually via eBay's Sell your item form. You can also complete the whole listing process without being connected to the internet. After you've created your listing templates within Turbo Lister you can either send the listings live to site or send them to your Selling Manager inventory.

Once you've downloaded the tool you will open it to the Turbo Lister home screen (see figure 25.6). Most of the instructions for using Turbo Lister will be based on this home screen.

Figure 25.6: the Turbo Lister home screen

Creating inventory using Turbo Lister

There are a number of ways to create inventory quickly using Turbo Lister. First, you can create an individual listing and simply duplicate it multiple times but make changes to tailor for specific products. Let's create a new listing together.

Creating a new listing using Turbo Lister

☐ Click **New** then click <u>Create New Item</u>.

☐ On the next page (see figure 25.7, p. 183) enter all of the relevant listing information, starting with item title.

☐ Choose the most relevant category for your item.

☐ You have the option of including the product number, which is usually the barcode number on the back of the product.

(continued)

Creating a new listing using Turbo Lister *(cont'd)*

☐ Under 'Details', click *Edit* to check for relevant item specifics relating to the product you're listing. Complete these as per previous examples in this chapter.

☐ Click *Click to insert picture* to upload a photo saved to your computer.

☐ Enter a complete product description under the heading 'Description'. Click *Description builder* to enter HTML.

☐ Further down the page, scroll to add a custom label your buyers cannot see (optional).

☐ On the right of the page under the 'Selling format' heading, complete your format, start price, quantity and duration details.

☐ Choose if you would like to add one of eBay's listing upgrades under the heading (this will generally attract an additional fee).

☐ Next, under 'Postage options' specify all of the methods you offer, including cost, handling time and international options.

☐ Select your chosen payment methods.

☐ Click *Edit* next to one of the 'Instructions and policies' for instructions visible to the buyer, your returns policy and blocked buyers.

☐ Click *Save* to create an individual listing or *Save as template* to use this template to create multiple product listings.

Now go back to your Turbo Lister home screen. You'll see that you have a new item or new template saved under the heading 'Inventory' on the left (in this example, we have saved both a listing and a template—see figure 25.8).

Figure 25.7: creating a new item in Turbo Lister

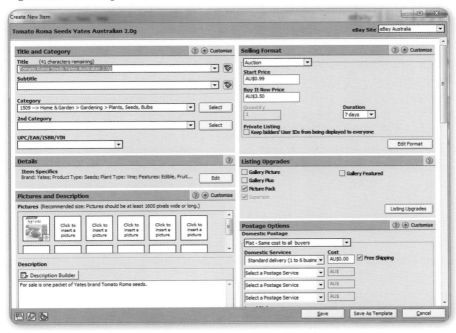

Figure 25.8: inventory in Turbo Lister

Listing your products and managing inventory

To duplicate a listing, simply click Duplicate just above the item title, choose how many duplicates you would like to make then click OK. Your inventory will automatically multiply to show your chosen number of exactly the same listing. Now you can edit each listing to make it product specific. To do this either double-click each listing to go to the edit item screen, as outlined previously in this chapter, or right-click any listing then click Enable inline editing. This will allow you to double-click any listing and edit the information right there on your inventory screen. Note you can also click Edit at the very top of the screen to edit item specifics, or search and replace specific information within your listing. Highlight multiple listings by using Control on your keyboard + click on your mouse, then right-click then click Edit Multiple items. Any changes you make to the edit item screen will apply to all highlighted listings.

If you created a template, you will need to create an item (or items) from that template. Click Templates under Inventory on the left (see figure 25.8). Highlight your chosen template then click Item from template. Choose the folder the item will be saved in then click OK. Complete the edit item screen as in the example earlier in this chapter.

You can also create multiple items by accessing eBay's product catalogue. As mentioned previously, not all products are covered by the catalogue, but it's worth checking regularly as this method of creating inventory will save you considerable time and effort. Let's complete this inventory-building process together.

Creating inventory using Turbo Lister

☐ Click New then Multiple items with pre-filled item information.

☐ Choose the eBay site you wish to list your products on then click Next.

☐ On the next screen, select the product type from the drop-down box (if your category is not listed here, there is no matching product in eBay's product catalogue), then enter the relevant product information in the fields below and choose your selling format (see figure 25.9). Click Add more items to upload multiple product types. Click Next.

☐ Turbo Lister will now reference the eBay product catalogue to detect whether there are any products to match the information you have entered. If there are matching products, check the relevant one(s) then click Save. These will automatically be added to your Inventory.

Figure 25.9: listing multiple items in Turbo Lister

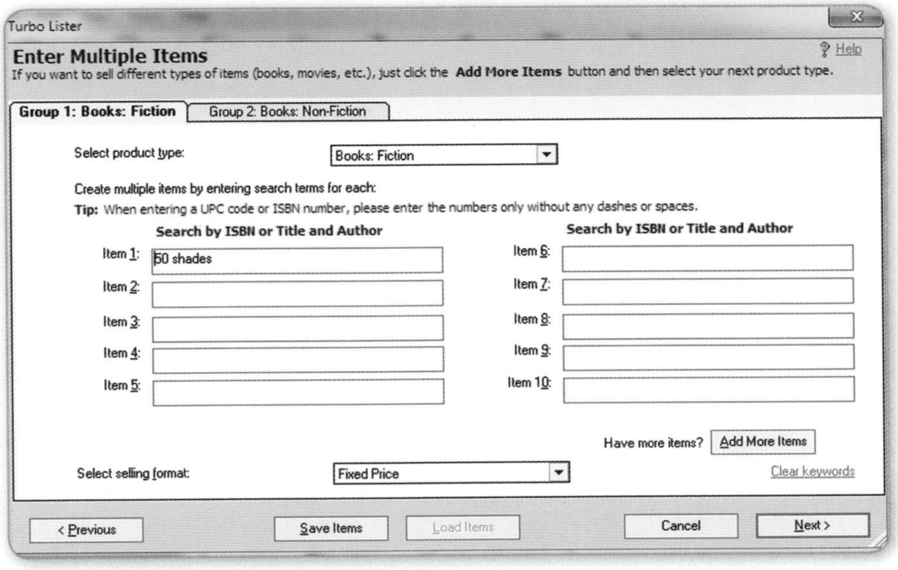

The final way to create inventory using Turbo Lister is to upload a file saved to your computer (usually a CSV file).

> ## Download your listing
>
> Before creating an extensive inventory, it is advisable to create one listing in Turbo Lister then download it so you can be sure you are formatting your inventory in the correct Turbo Lister layout. To download your listing, highlight it within your inventory then click File and Export Selected items. You can then use that example to create multiple listings, or ensure your existing product inventory matches the correct formatting.

To import a file of inventory, click File then Import items then From file to access documents on your computer, or From eBay if you would like to upload listings you have already created using eBay's Sell your item form or Selling Manager.

Once you're happy with the inventory in Turbo Lister, you then need to upload your listings to eBay. Simply highlight those you wish to send live to the site then click Add to upload, or highlight the listing(s) then use your

Listing your products and managing inventory

mouse to slide them into the Waiting To Upload folder (see figure 25.10). Next go to Waiting To Upload under 'Inventory' in the left navigation pane and click Upload all to send all listings live to eBay; or use the drop-down arrow next to Upload all and click Upload selected (only those you have highlighted), or Upload to selling manager (which creates an inventory in Selling Manager but does not send the listings live to eBay). You can also click Schedule to choose a different start time for your listings or Calculate fees to total the fees you will pay on eBay. The same functionalities can be accessed by clicking Tools at the top of the page.

Figure 25.10: uploading inventory via Turbo Lister

You can organise your inventory on Turbo Lister by creating different folders for different product types. You do this by clicking File then New then Folder, or by using the drop-down arrow next to New and clicking Create new folder. You can manage much of the content on Turbo Lister as on any Windows-based desktop — cutting, copying, pasting and sliding with ease.

Click Help at the top of the home screen for more information on how to use Turbo Lister effectively.

Create bulk listings with eBay's API

If you have an existing website, product catalogue or spreadsheet of product information, you can access eBay's API (Application Programming Interface) to create bulk listings. It requires high-level technical expertise, but the API allows you to interact with eBay's database directly using a language known as XML (eXtensible Markup Language), which affords you a customisable, specialised way to list on the site or extract other information from eBay specific to your business's needs. You can access the API directly by joining eBay's developer's network (known as X.Commerce) or using an existing developer's program to upload your data. You can find more information at www.x.com/developers/ebay. Click on Use cases then Large merchant services then choose the most relevant option for you. To find existing developers go to www.x.com/developers/developer-directory. If you don't really know what you're doing and don't have access to a website developer, it's best to employ an existing eBay developer to address your business's requirements.

This is the most efficient and cost-effective way of uploading more than a few hundred products—up to millions. You will need to thoroughly test your access to the API on a small number of listings before ramping up to thousands or more.

Manage your inventory with Magento

Another option is to consider running your online business via a third-party tool that allows you to list on eBay. In other words, third-party tools manage your inventory across multiple channels, including your own website(s), eBay and some other marketplaces such as Amazon (www.amazon.com). A number of options exist, ranging from a small monthly fee to a per-sale percentage fee. Among the most popular is Magento (www.magento.com), an eBay-owned website management tool that allows you to list your products on multiple sites and manage all sales.

Magento has tailored tools to suit your requirements as a business. For smaller businesses looking to open or upgrade an online store, the recommended product is Magento Go. Hosted and managed by Magento, Magento Go does not require any specific software download to operate. It's basically a template-design website solution where you pick and choose from the options available. You can customise your own design without needing to know website programming languages such as HTML. Product features of Magento Go include tools to:

- create your own category and product display features
- accept multiple payment methods
- create your own website at the same time as synching it to eBay, so you increase your chances of attracting additional buyers to your products
- set prices in multiple currencies for international buyers
- run comprehensive reporting and analytics
- provide advanced shipping calculator options for your buyers
- automatically optimise for search engine rankings
- provide complete inventory management
- support advanced marketing and promotion
- integrate live chat and telephone customer support.

Starting at $15 and rising to up to $125 per month, Magento Go gives you options for 100 products up to 10000, up to 30 administrative accounts, and options for 24/7 support.

If you're looking for a more advanced solution, then Magento Enterprise may be right for you. With more flexibility for advanced business-specific solutions, it gives you complete control over your website's look and feel so it can be a total reflection of your brand. Core product features include:

- advanced search engine optimisation
- customer segmentation
- targeted promotions and merchandising
- vouchers and coupons for specific customers
- customer-assisted shopping
- returns management solution
- customer rewards points
- gift registry
- multiple stores from one Magento licence
- mobile commerce
- optimised speed and performance.

Magento Enterprise Edition has annual fees starting at around $15 000. There is also Magento Enterprise Premium fees, with around $50 000 per year (this includes increased support from Magento plus professional training). Magento Enterprise Premium is aimed at existing large and complex business structures, so if you're not currently online, or if you need a fully comprehensive online arm to your existing business, this could be the right option for you.

Other third-party listing tools

If you don't want to use Magento there are other options that provide similar types of functionalities.

Channel Advisor offers a complete online sales solution, including uploading your inventory to marketplaces such as eBay and Amazon as well as comparison shopping websites and paid search programs (advertising on sites such as Google), your own website and campaigns on social media sites such as Facebook. Fees vary depending on your specific requirements but usually entail a per-sale percentage. For more information visit www.channeladvisor.com.au.

e.pages is a cloud-based web management tool that allows you to design your own website from available templates and upload your inventory to shopping comparison websites and marketplaces such as eBay and Amazon, and to optimise your search engine rankings. In Australia the service is offered by eCorner (more information can be found at www.ecorner.com.au).

Many more options can be found by conducting an internet search or visiting eBay's Developer directory. It's a good idea to review your options carefully before committing to a subscription or longer term contract with a specific provider, and ask to see examples of other businesses using that solution. If possible, speak to a user and get their feedback on the pros and cons. Check for options that are standalone or give you the option of running the program yourself without losing any of the information or operations you have paid for.

Chapter 26
Best match—visibility in eBay search

Best match is eBay's default search algorithm. As explained in parts II and III of this book, it is the way the vast majority of buyers' search results are ordered. Product placement is one of the classic tenets of retail, so on eBay having your listings appear as close to the top of search results as possible is one of the fundamental requirements for having a profitable business. You will be in constant competition with other sellers to get to the top of the list, and while there are no sure-fire guarantees (and eBay will never release the finer details of its algorithm), there are some key factors you should consider to help increase the visibility of your products in an eBay search.

Recent sales

The more products you sell from within one listing, the more eBay recognises that listing as being in demand and popular with buyers. Popularity is one of the main measurements of the Best match algorithm. For this reason, you should consider implementing the following tactics wherever possible.

List at a fixed price using multiquantity *and* multivariant. In other words, as auctions are limited to one of each product per listing, take advantage of fixed price, which allows you to list large quantities of products in each listing. Further, using multivariant (including multiple sizes, colours and styles, for example) within the same fixed price listing gives you even greater opportunity to sell more products.

List in longer duration formats such as stores' 30-day format. The longer your listing is live on eBay, the more buyers will see it and the more sales are likely to result.

It's better to continue relisting the same original listing than to create a new one from scratch, as your recent sales history will carry over.

Be price competitive. The more competitively priced you are, the more buyers you are likely to attract and the more sales you are likely to achieve. This includes the *total* cost of buying from you, including postage, handling, insurance, return shipping and any other costs.

Be professional and courteous. If your listings are professionally designed and the language contained within them is courteous, buyers will be more inclined to buy from you. Some buyers are even willing to trade off the lowest price for peace of mind.

Feedback and DSR ratings can also influence a buyer's willingness to purchase from you.

Relevance

As well as recognising recent sales, increased visibility is given to those listings considered most relevant to a given buyer search. There is a fine line between being relevant and scrambling for attention.

Carefully choose the most relevant category for your product and do not rush into making that decision. For example, there may be a lawnmowers category but also a lawnmower accessories category, and a grass-catcher is a better match for the latter category.

Use strong, popular keywords in your item title. The research you conducted at the beginning of part IV will have helped you create the ideal listing title. Make sure you do not keyword spam, or, in other words, use keywords not related to your item. Misusing keywords can contravene eBay's policies, which can result in the cancellation of your listing. Even using broader keywords, while not essentially against policy, may affect your relevancy score, because if someone is searching for a wallet and you include the keyword wallet ('wallet sized business card holder') in your title, your listing will receive an impression for every buyer search for 'wallet'. If you receive no, or few, clicks as a result, your relevancy score will be compromised and this may affect the visibility of your products in eBay searches.

Finally, make sure you use eBay's item specifics, because these also help eBay understand which listings are most relevant for a buyer's search.

Seller performance

The feedback and detailed ratings you receive from buyers will directly affect the performance of your listings in Best match. If your scores or ratings fall below a given threshold, your search visibility will be impacted. Similarly, if you contravene eBay's policies, receive too many complaints from buyers or do not pay your eBay fees, your seller performance score will be low. For this reason, consider the following guidelines.

Aim for inclusion in the eBay Top-rated Seller (eTRS) program because this may have an impact on your placement within Best match. eTRS status is awarded to those sellers who provide a higher level of service, such as a minimum number of 1- and 2-rated DSR scores, a minimum average of DSR scores and a minimum number of transactions. You will also carry the eTRS icon in your listings and on the search results page, which encourages buyer trust and could help with your sales volume, so it's well worth aspiring to be included in the program (inclusion happens automatically and is updated every month).

Create clear, concise listings so your buyers can easily understand what they are buying and your terms of trade. You need to set very clear buyer expectations and avoid surprises, so be thorough but avoid rambling or including too much information, as buyers will skip over it.

Set a clear buyer expectation for postage and handling time and stick to it. If there are any unforeseen delays, contact your buyer to explain.

Communicate with your buyers throughout the sales process. Let them know when payment has been received, when their products have been shipped and when they can expect to receive them.

Leave positive, encouraging feedback for your buyers. If you receive any negative feedback from them (and it's almost inevitable that you will receive a negative rating at some point in your eBay business's lifetime), take the time to learn from the experience and put appropriate measures in place to help ensure the same problem does not occur again.

Be aware of eBay's policies—ignorance is not an acceptable excuse for contravening them. If you break eBay's rules you will eventually be caught, and breaking rules consistently not only will adversely affect your visibility in an eBay search but could lead to suspension or expulsion from the site.

If buyers complain to eBay that they have not received their item, it's not as described or it's faulty, always provide a satisfactory solution for them and ensure that the case is marked as resolved in eBay's resolution centre.

Finally, pay your eBay invoices on time—choose an automatic payment method (for more information see chapter 28).

Postage and other services

Sellers who charge an amount for postage that is proportionally higher than the item price, or is much higher than the average in their category, may have their visibility impacted, depending on the rules at the time. Broad principles for providing outstanding buyer service include the following:

• Don't charge more for postage than you need to.

• Consider offering free postage options.

• Offer a tracked shipping method.

• Offer returns, preferably 30 days or more.

• Minimise your handling time—reduce it to same day or next day wherever possible.

• Offer an expedited shipping option for your buyers.

How new listings are treated

If you're a new seller, or have created a new listing, you may not have enough history for eBay to score you on these factors. In this case, new listings are given the same number of impressions as the best-performing listings and have a small window of opportunity to attract the same amount of buyer interest. If they are unable to match the performance of the highest scoring listings, their search visibility is impacted. For this reason it's important for you to understand who the top performers are in the most popular searches for your products and to do your best to emulate those strategies that buyers like best.

How to improve your Best match performance

eBay has a tool called the Seller Dashboard that helps explain your performance in Best match, among other things. To view your performance, click My eBay at the top of any page then click Account then Seller dashboard. Within My eBay also click Applications then Listing analytics to view the performance of your active listings and best practices within your category.

You can also conduct an internet search for tips from others on how to optimise your listings for Best match. Some are very helpful while others are a little hit and miss, so use them selectively.

iPhone iPad On the iPhone, click Settings then click your user ID to see your ratings and recent feedback. On the iPad, click the *Navigation* tab at top left then click your user ID.

Best match summary

There is no golden rule to follow to ensure you are the best performer in Best match. You may find that you have changed nothing about your listings or your performance but suddenly start slipping in search results — this may be because there has been a change in your competitors' performance and you're not keeping up.

Remember finally that Best match is a comparison tool. It simply looks at every single listing corresponding to a buyer's search and orders them according to the factors outlined in this chapter, among others. You will receive one of the best positions in search results only if Best match deems you to be among the best and most popular sellers, so you need to continually assess your competition and ensure you remain as good as, or better than, others in your category.

Best match also helps rationalise the number of auctions and fixed price listings on each page. Remember from the introduction to this book that more than 80 per cent of all bought items on eBay are from fixed price listings. Best match helps ensure that the most popular formats within each category are given the correct weighting.

While the algorithm continues to change almost monthly, striving to be the best seller with the most popular products in your category should help ensure you maintain a positive ranking in search results.

Chapter 27
Opening a store and marketing options

Your eBay store is effectively your own branded website within eBay. You receive a unique URL (website address) and can design and brand your store any way you choose. eBay buyers are able to search your entire store for every item you have for sale, save your store as a favourite, and view other information about your business such as terms of trade and frequently asked questions. For eBay sellers, stores come packed with excellent marketing functions, discounted listing and other fees, and help add a higher level of professionalism to your eBay business. For a fraction of the price of creating your own website, you can have your eBay store up and running in a matter of minutes. Better still, your store will be referenced by search engines such as Google, helping with the fourth P of retail, *promotion*.

Subscribe to a store

Depending on the eBay site you subscribe from, you will have two or three store subscription levels to choose from. Each level has a different monthly subscription fee, different functionalities and different listing fees (listing fees are covered in the next chapter). To subscribe to a store, or upgrade, click Customer Support at the top of any eBay page and type 'store' in the help search box, then click *Search*.

Table 27.1 shows the costs and some of the additional benefits of each store level on the Australian site.

Table 27.1: eBay store costs and benefits

	Basic store	Featured store	Anchor store
Monthly subscription	$19.95	$49.95	$499.95
Additional customisable pages	5	10	15
Advanced store traffic reporting		✓	✓
Selling Manager Pro free	✓	✓	✓
Sales Reports Plus	✓	✓	✓

Once you have subscribed to a store, you'll be able to access it any time by clicking the *red door icon* that appears next to your user ID. Once in your store, scroll down to the very bottom of the page and click <u>Seller, manage store</u>. This takes you to the Manage My Store screen, the central hub for all things related to your store (see figure 27.1).

Figure 27.1: the Manage My Store hub

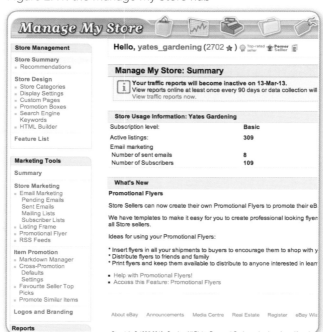

One of the most important links you will need to use on this page is Feature list in the navigation area on the left of Manage My Store. This will take you to a list of most of your store's operations.

Choose a store name, description and logo

As outlined earlier in part IV, it's important that your store name reflect your eBay user ID and that all of your branding is consistent on eBay. While your user ID cannot contain spaces, store names can, so bear this in mind. To create or update your store name and description, click Feature list then Store information. You can also access this by clicking Display settings in the left navigation area of Manage My Store then clicking Change next to the relevant section. Enter the relevant information on the next screen then click *Save Settings*. Note that your store description will be referenced by internet search engines such as Google, so it's important to use strong, highly relevant keywords in sentence form, not just a list of words. Your store name will be used to create your unique URL, so make sure it is simple to remember.

eBay has a selection of pre-designed logos for you to choose from for your store. These are a little generic and basic and it is much more professional to add your own logo. This logo will appear on selected communications to your buyers and in other areas of the site, so upload a high-resolution version of your logo in colour. It must be 310 × 90 pixels, so have your logo professionally resized to avoid it looking stretched or of poor quality. You can upload your logo along with your store name and description to the store information page.

Choose a store design

When you subscribe to eBay stores you can choose from eBay's basic designs, which is the simplest way to brand your store. These store templates have been on eBay for quite some time, though, so they can appear a little dated. Take your time to choose the best combination of background colours, font styles and colours, and you will be able to create something that is unique and broadly aligned to your brand personality. To create your design, click Display Settings in the left navigation area of Manage My Store then click Edit current theme or Change to another theme.

On the next page you will be able to change your store's colour palette and font options for text that appears on the page. Alternatively, you'll be able to pick from among eBay's pre-designed themes and layouts. Make sure you choose colours that complement your brand.

You also have the option of entering highly polished HTML (web design language) to design a store that is modern and unique and embraces any style element you like. You can teach yourself HTML from books or the internet, but a moderate to advanced skill level will get the job done much faster and much more professionally. It's well worth considering outsourcing the design of your eBay store (for consistency, the same design can then be applied to your eBay listing template). Again, you could consider contacting a design school to employ a student to complete this for you, and an internet search for 'eBay store design' will show many other options. One of the most experienced companies working to design unique stores for Australian businesses is the UK-based Frooition, which can design your store (and listing template) usually within a few weeks and usually for a few thousand dollars. For more information visit www.frooition.com/au/ — though it's a considerable investment you will not be disappointed with the end result, and neither will your buyers.

If you're entering your own HTML, choose Custom pages in the left navigation area of Manage My Store then click Create new page then click 1 Text Section / HTML. Click **Continue** then enter your HTML in the Stores HTML Builder field and click **Continue**. Carefully review your content then click **Save and publish**.

Finally, on the display settings page, choose which other options you wish to display within your store:

• *Show search box*—displays a search box that allows buyers to search your entire store for particular products

• *Show categories*—displays a list of customer-created categories for your store (more on this later in the chapter)

• *Show buyer display options*—allows your buyer to view your store in a number of different layouts

• *Show store pages*—gives buyers a list of all pages in your store

• *Store page header*—adds your chosen header (or customised header) at the top of your store

- *eBay header style* — for highest level stores, allows you to minimise the eBay header at the top of your store to encourage buyers to search only your inventory rather than the whole site

- *Item display* — choose how your products will be displayed within your store (list view is a single column of photos to the left, listing titles to the right: gallery view is a three-column format with larger photos above listing titles)

- *Compatibility* — for selected products with catalogue information, display that information in the item's subtitle.

Create store categories

While every one of your products must be placed within one of eBay's specified categories, not every product falls neatly into eBay's lists. Store categories give you the opportunity to create your own category structure to help your buyers find your products more quickly. Buyers can access your category structure only once they are inside your store, or from a listing frame applied to your listings (more on that later in this chapter).

Click Store categories under Store design in the left navigation area of Manage my store to create your store's structure. Click *Add Category* on the right to create a new category. Check the box next to each category and use the buttons at the bottom of the page to *Rename*, *Move category* or *Delete*. You can create as many as 300 unique categories over three different levels (for example, Clothing > Women's Clothing > Dresses), and each one of your listings can be assigned to one or two of your store categories. If you have no listings active within a particular category, it will not appear within your store.

The trick here is to think like your most frequent customers — how do they like to browse your products, or what kinds of product attributes provide the most logical way to structure your categories? Don't overwhelm your buyers with too many options, and never use a structure that's so generic your products could appear in several categories at once. Always double-check your spelling and structure your categories either alphabetically or in a logical retail store–like manner. You should also consider creating special categories that attract more attention from buyers, such as discounted lines, new releases or other special deals.

Opening a store and marketing options

Store marketing tools

Don't assume that simply getting your listings live on eBay is all you need to do to secure healthy repeat business. As we've discussed previously, one of the keys to retail and eBay business success is promotion. Stores come with a host of marketing features to help you attract more buyers both from within, and outside, eBay. Over the years, I've challenged most sellers I've met on whether they are utilising their eBay store to its fullest potential. Most sellers are not, and yet doing so is one way you may be able to get ahead of your competition. It will take a little time and patience to establish each marketing function, but once done, most remain on permanently until you decide to turn them off again. Each one of the following links can be clicked in the left navigation area of Manage my store.

Promotion Boxes lets you create special promotional displays and add them to various pages within your store. Click *Create new promotion box* and choose from one of the eBay templates to promote specific listings, link to other areas within your store or create your own promotion box using HTML. Follow the prompts to choose where your box will appear. A free third-party product I use to create an animated banner at the top of my store (see figure 27.2) is Scrolleo. For more information, visit www.scrolleo.com.

Search engine keywords is the primary way for you to get your store noticed by buyers outside eBay. Search engines such as Google reference these keywords and provide links to your eBay store if they are deemed sufficiently relevant to a buyer's search. Choose keywords that are specific to your products, brand and categories. Note that search engine keywords are also automatically applied to each of your store categories, so creating your own category structure is an additional way of driving traffic to your store.

With HTML builder you can create HTML links to your products, store pages, newsletter subscriptions or your store search, and choose from a simple text link or incorporate product images for a more professional design.

Figure 27.2: HTML-designed store with custom promotion box

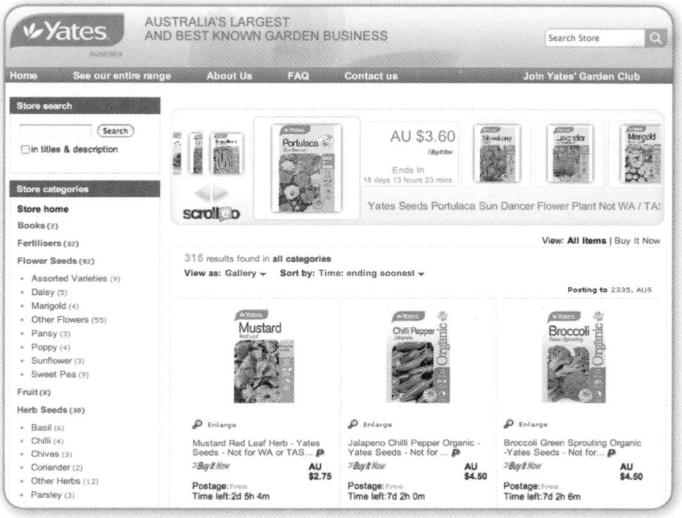

Listing frame adds your store header, logo, categories, links to sign up for newsletters (more information on this later in this chapter) and a search box for your store to all of your eBay listings. This is a great way to capture engaged shoppers and lure them into your store to buy more than a single item.

RSS feeds lets you choose to activate your listings for really simple syndication (RSS) feeds used by shopping comparison and other websites for instant updates to potential buyers.

Use Markdown manager to reduce the price of all or selected listings by a set dollar amount or percentage for a specified length of time. Sales can be one to 45 days in duration and the number of listings you can reduce the price on varies from 250 to 5000, depending on your store level. You can also reduce postage costs as another type of markdown promotion. These work best when incorporated into promotion boxes or email marketing.

Cross promotion allows you to choose to have your listings promoted to interested buyers (those who bid on your auctions or complete checkout). eBay will automatically display your chosen products to that buyer. You can also choose which types of listings will be displayed and in which format.

Favourite seller top picks functions so that if a buyer selects you as one of their favourite sellers, your top (selected) items will be displayed on their top picks page and email. You can choose between automatic and manual selection. This is a great way to promote newly listed products or products on sale.

With Promote similar items you can choose to have your listings promoted alongside similar sellers on certain eBay pages, including end-of-item notices, watch notification emails and closed item pages. Checking any of these boxes will display your listings on similar sellers' listing pages but will also display similar sellers on your pages.

Communicate with buyers

Having a store means you can communicate with your buyers in a number of efficient ways. Only stores give you this added functionality, creating more opportunities for repeat business from loyal customers. eBay businesses that invest the time to make their marketing communications more effective are reaping the rewards from dedicated active buyers. The danger here is doing a less than professional job, which will serve only to distract your buyers or discourage them from returning to your store.

Marketing is a specific skill and requires talent, dedication, and a sound knowledge of your customers and their requirements. If you are investing in communicating directly with your buyers via eBay stores, consider asking a marketing expert for advice or to provide feedback on your marketing plans. Most marketing provides a lesson in hit-and-miss, and you should be prepared to learn from mistakes rather than have mistakes dissuade you from trying alternative programs. What works one week for your buyers may not work the next. The important thing is to create direct, measurable campaigns that lead to customer loyalty and increased sales.

From the left navigation area of Manage My Store, click on one of the following links.

Email marketing enables you to include links in your store for subscribing to newsletters (as outlined earlier in this chapter). Make your subscription link prominent in your store header or on your store homepage. Once you have subscribers, click Email marketing then click *Create email* to choose from one of eBay's template emails to highlight specific products to a selection or all of your subscribers. On the create email page, click Custom to enter your own HTML and design a unique, more professional email for your buyers. You can have emails sent automatically on a regular basis (such as weekly or fortnightly) or send them manually each time. The number of emails you can send each month varies from 100 to 4000, depending on your store subscription level. Exceeding your allocation results in a charge of 1c per email.

On marketing emails

When sending emails it's crucial to choose the right subject line for your buyers. Make the subject line as enticing as possible because you want your email recipients to open the mail and then click on one of your listings. Consider sending emails only for special events such as sales, new release promotions, subscriber anniversaries or to welcome new subscribers. Keep your content minimal—focus on your products and don't distract your buyers with too much text. Triple-check your spelling before sending and, most important, monitor your email open rates. Keep track of what types of emails work best for your buyers and strive to continually improve your open rates.

Back on the email marketing page, click *Create mailing list* to collect your subscribers into specific groups so you can choose to send certain types of buyers different types of emails. On your email marketing summary page, eBay will keep a list of all of the emails you have sent, how many customers opened the email and the date it was sent. You can click on the links to see the email and duplicate to send similar emails in the future.

Using the Promotional flyer link you can design and print a brochure-type communication to include in the packages you send to your buyers. Choose one of the eBay themes or your store's colour scheme to create a flyer showcasing some of your most popular products, and choose additional information to include, such as your returns policy. If including flyers in your packaging, print only in colour and make sure it looks professional and has a *call to action* for your buyers. A call to action is an enticement to your buyers to visit your store, such as price reductions or new releases.

The Logos and branding link enables you to add your logo and brand to some of eBay's automatic emails to your buyers. We will cover this area of the site, 'Manage communications with buyers', later, in chapter 29. Only store subscribers have the option of branding eBay's communications with their own colours and logo.

On privacy laws

Be mindful of privacy laws in Australia. If a buyer communicates directly with you, or you need to communicate in the course of completing a transaction, this is generally acceptable business practice. If you trawl through previous transaction summaries and then add your buyers to an unsolicited email campaign, you may be infringing privacy laws. The simplest rule to follow is if your buyers have not asked to hear from you, you should proceed with caution. Refer to the Australian government's website at www.privacy.gov.au for more information.

Another important feature of stores is a function called Holiday hold. This can be used if you're a sole operator or all your staff are on leave and you need to close your store for a period of time. Holiday hold still allows buyers to browse your store but clearly labels your business as closed for holidays and will not allow new buyers to purchase from you during the period on hold. Your previous buyers will still be allowed to purchase from you but will receive a message that you are on leave and to expect a delay before receiving their products. Click Feature list in the left navigation area of Manage my store then click Holiday hold to activate this feature.

Stores reporting

A key component of operating a successful and profitable business is reporting. Reports can help you quickly identify your business's strengths and weaknesses, giving you an opportunity to capitalise on the former and improve on the latter. We'll cover stores reporting later, in chapter 32.

Unsubscribing from your store

Should you ever wish to change your store subscription level or close your store altogether, you can do so by clicking Manage subscriptions near the bottom of the left navigation area of Manage my store.

Other marketing options

While your eBay store is one of the primary ways to get your products noticed more on eBay, there are other options outside of having a store that will boost your profile considerably.

eBay Deals and Sales

As covered in part II, eBay Deals and Sales are a great way to showcase your most popular items, particularly when you're able to discount them to an unbeatable price. Most products featured in eBay Deals and Sales must offer a minimum discount off retail, and most must have a free shipping option. Buyers love Deals and Sales—they're among the most popular pages on eBay and its mobile apps. Buyers can also choose to subscribe to daily alerts every time a new product is listed for sale. Participation in Deals and Sales is at eBay's discretion, so make sure you have new, branded, discounted items and your feedback and DSR scores are above average. You can see what is currently on sale by clicking eBay Deals at top left of the eBay homepage.

eBay also operates group deals on individual products at unbeatable prices (usually electronics and home wares). Group deals activate only when a minimum number of buyers have committed to purchase, so you can be assured that your profit margins will be maintained if you need to purchase the product in bulk from your suppliers.

You can find out more about submitting your products to Deals and Sales and the guidelines that must be followed by scrolling to the bottom of the Deals page and clicking Frequently asked questions.

On-eBay advertising

Another way to get your brand noticed on eBay is to purchase advertising on the site. While Google text links appear at the bottom of some search pages, the eBay advertising team can offer prime visual advertisements on key pages throughout the site. You can speak to the team about purchasing selected keywords and other ways to target your campaigns to the most relevant buyers. To find out more and discuss rates, click Advertise at the bottom right of any eBay page.

Off-eBay advertising

Once your eBay business is operating and coping with the demand, you could choose to advertise your business on websites outside eBay or via offline channels. Because each eBay store has a unique URL, you can direct potential buyers straight to your store. Google is the best place to start looking and offers starter advertising packages via its Adwords program. You cannot purchase the keyword 'eBay', but you will be able to bid for other keywords associated with the products you sell.

You could also consider advertising your eBay business in niche publications where your buyers are most likely to be found. Use only your own logo and branding. Do not use any eBay logos or eBay intellectual property unless you have express permission to do so from the company.

eBay and PayPal fees

Now we've covered how to establish a professional presence on eBay it's important to understand how eBay and PayPal charges sellers. Over the years I've met many sellers who have criticised eBay fees, but in my opinion they represent great value for money when you take into account the 7 million–plus Australians who visit the site every month and the other options online businesses have, such as creating their own website from scratch and paying for an effective search engine marketing campaign (such as Google advertising). I think of the overheads my own father had to outlay in creating his small (offline) business. Had eBay been around back then, how much more efficient his business would have been, and how many more potential customers he'd have been able to tap into 24 hours per day, seven days a week!

Whatever your view on the value of eBay's and PayPal's fees, it's important to consider all the benefits selling on the site brings. If you investigate other options you may find cheaper alternatives, but you'll struggle to find a larger customer base than eBay's. eBay fees tend to change on a fairly regular basis—at least annually—so make sure you continue to check the site for the latest information. As covered in chapter 22, eBay and PayPal fees are one component of your cost per sale. Look at all the options offered by both companies to ensure you have optimised your profit and elected to pay the lowest fees possible.

Fees also vary depending on the site on which you list your products. If you want your products to appear on the US site in US dollars, for example, you need to list directly on eBay.com, and the same applies for the UK (eBay.co.uk). Tables 28.1 to 28.3 (pp. 211–213) outline the relevant fees for each of the three major English-language sites.

Pay and understand your eBay fees

The most efficient way to pay your eBay fees is to establish an automatic payment plan. This way, you need never worry about missing an invoice and having restrictions placed on your account. To update your payment method, click <u>My eBay</u> at the top of any eBay page, then click <u>Account</u> then <u>Seller account</u> (see figure 28.1). Next, under the heading 'Payment methods for seller fees' click <u>Change</u>. You can also make a one-time payment using PayPal or another method by clicking <u>one-time payment</u>.

Figure 28.1: the Seller fees information page in My eBay

This is also the page where you can view invoices for the past 18 months. Use the **Select Invoice** drop-down on the right to choose a month, then click **Go**. You can download invoices to save to your computer for future reference. The account summary in the middle of the page shows your eBay fees summary since your last invoice. Click one of the links below the total to see:

• <u>All account activity</u>—summarises all of your selling, fees, credits and payment activities

• <u>Fees</u>—shows the total eBay and PayPal fees paid for the period

• <u>Credits</u>—outlines any credits that have been made, for example because of unpaid items

• <u>Payments and refunds</u>—summarises all of the payments you have made to eBay and any refunds made to your account (as may occur if eBay ends your listing for a policy violation, for example).

Fee structures on eBay sites

There are four main categories of seller, each allocated a different fee structure as shown in the following tables. The first one applies to all sellers who do not subscribe to an eBay store; the next three correspond with the store subscription level you have chosen.

Table 28.1: fees on eBay Australia

Subscription per month		No store — N/A		Basic store — $19.95			Featured store — $49.95			Anchor store — $499.95	
Format (# in brackets is listing per month)		Auction and fixed price (1–40)	Auction and fixed price (40+)	Auction	Fixed price and collect. auction (1–80)	Fixed price (80+)	Auction	Fixed price and collect. auction (1–200)	Fixed price (200+)	Auction	Fixed price
Insertion fees	Collectables	$0.00			$0.00			$0.00			$0.00
	$0.01–$19.99		$0.50	$0.50		$1.00	$0.50		$1.00	$0.50	
	$20.00–$99.99		$1.50	$1.50			$1.50			$1.50	
	$100.00 +		$3.50	$3.50			$3.50			$3.50	
	Media										
	$0.01–$19.99		$0.50	$0.50		$0.05	$0.50		$0.05	$0.50	
	$20.00–$99.99		$1.50	$1.50			$1.50			$1.50	
	$100.00 +		$3.50	$3.50			$3.50			$3.50	
	Other										
	$0.01 – $19.99		$0.50	$0.50		$0.50	$0.50		$0.20	$0.50	
	$20.00–$99.99		$1.50	$1.50			$1.50			$1.50	
	$100.00 +		$3.50	$3.50			$3.50			$3.50	
Final value fee	Collectables, fashion, electronics accessories, media	9.90%		9.50%			8.50%			7.50%	
	Business and industrial, home and garden, lifestyle, car parts and accessories, electronics (<$200)			8.00%			7.00%			6.00%	
	Electronics (> $200)			6.00%			5.00%			4.00%	
	Cap	$250									

eBay and PayPal fees

The New eBay

Table 28.2: fees on eBay US

Subscription per month	No store		Basic store			Featured store			Anchor store		
	N/A		$19.95 (if paid monthly) / $15.95 (if paid annually)			$59.95 (if paid monthly) / $49.95 (if paid annually)			$199.95 (if paid monthly) / $179.95 (if paid annually)		
Format (# in brackets is listing per month)	Auction and fixed price (1–50)	Auction and fixed price (50 +)	Auction and fixed price (1–150)	Auction (150+)	Fixed price (150+)	Auction and fixed price (1–500)	Auction (500+)	Fixed price (500+)	Auction and fixed price (1–2500)	Auction (2500+)	Fixed price (2500+)
Insertion Fees	$0.00	$0.30	$0.00	$0.25	$0.20	$0.00	$0.15	$0.10	$0.00	$0.10	$0.05

Final Value Fee:

Category	No store	Featured store
Computers, video game consoles, business and industrial capital equipment	10.00%	4.00%
Tech devices, car parts: electronics, tech other		6.00%
Musical instruments, coins		7.00%
Car parts		8.00%
All other categories		9.00%
Cap		$250*

* cap does not apply to Business & Industrial capital equipment

Table 28.3: fees eBay UK

		No Store		Basic Store		Featured Store		Anchor Store	
Subscription per month		N/A		£14.99		£49.99		£349.99	
Format		Auction and fixed price (1–50)	Auction and fixed price (50+)	Auction	Fixed price	Auction	Fixed price	Auction	Fixed price
Insertion Fees	All Categories								
	£0.01 – £0.99	£0.00		£0.10		£0.10		£0.10	
	£1–£4.99	£0.15		£0.15		£0.15		£0.15	
	£5–£14.99	£0.25	$0.30	£0.25	£0.10	£0.25	£0.05	£0.25	£0.00
	£15–£29.99	£0.50		£0.50		£0.50		£0.50	
	£30–£99.99	£1.00		£1.00		£1.00		£1.00	
	£100+	£1.30		£1.30		£1.30		£1.30	
	Media								
	£0.01–£0.99	£0.00		£0.05	£0.10	£0.05	£0.05	£0.05	
	£1+	£0.10		£0.10		£0.10		£0.10	
Final Value Fee	Clothing, shoes, accessories	10.00%		11.00%					
	Media			8.00%					
	Car parts			7.00%					
	Technology			4.00%					
	All other categories			9.00%					

PayPal fees

If you accept PayPal as your payment method, additional fees apply to each item. PayPal fees vary for businesses, depending on the total value of goods sold where PayPal was the buyer's payment method (see table 28.4). Make sure you have applied for merchant rates. This is a once-only application and new fees will automatically apply once you have reached new turnover levels. Unlike eBay fees, if you sell your products on an overseas website (eBay or others) your standard Australian PayPal fees apply, as you are registered as an Australian business.

Table 28.4: PayPal fees

Monthly PayPal volume	Domestic payments (AU$)		Cross-border payments	
	Percentage fee	Fixed fee	Percentage fee	Fixed fee
Under $5000	2.4		3.4	
$5000.01–$15000	2.0	$0.30	3.0	Varies by currency*
$15000.01–$150000	1.5		2.5	
Over $150000	1.1		2.1	

*For more information and a complete list of PayPal fees, click Fees at the bottom of any PayPal page.

Paymate fees

Table 28.5 summarises the fees that will apply if you choose to accept Paymate for your eBay transactions.

Table 28.5: Paymate fees

Account type	Monthly fee	Monthly prepaid payment value*	Transaction fee**	
			Percentage	Fixed fee
Standard	nil	$0	2.475	
Regular	$8.25	$500	2.200	$0.55
Professional	$33.00	$2000	1.925	
Business	$165.00	$10000	1.650	

*You pay no fees until your transactions exceed this amount.
**On transactions exceeding your prepaid payment value
Note: Accepting payments in foreign currencies attracts a further 2.5 per cent charge.

Merchant credit card fees

If you accept credit card payments for your eBay transactions and process these yourself via a merchant credit-card processing facility, your business banking provider will be able to supply you with a list of the relevant fees. These generally vary from bank to bank and depend on the type of business account you have created. Speak to your bank manager to ensure you have optimised the fees you pay for all your business needs. It's wise to collect a variety of quotes from different institutions so you can be sure you're getting the best deal to suit your needs.

Planning a business
TOP 10

10 things you need to know about planning for a profitable eBay business

1   Complete your research thoroughly *before* you dive into starting an eBay business, to make sure there is an adequate profitable opportunity selling your chosen products on eBay.

2   Brand every aspect of your eBay business consistently — your brand should be clear across your ID, store, email address, listing information and marketing materials, for example.

3   Reduce your time overhead wherever possible. Constantly look for ways to reduce the time it takes to complete each of the tasks associated with running your eBay business.

4   Learn from others. Buy from your competitors both on and off eBay. Pay careful attention to what you need to emulate (or be better than) and what you need to avoid

5   Plan for growth. Completing a business plan is time consuming and can sometimes feel daunting, but I've seen too many eBay sellers fall into the trap of struggling to keep up with business because they have not planned adequately for future growth and their systems are unable to cope with the volume of buyers eBay can delivered. Taking your time to complete a comprehensive business plan will pay you dividends in the long run.

6   Learn something new. Every small business owner I know complains that there isn't enough time in the day to get everything done. This means finding time to teach yourself new information is very difficult. From day one, plan one to two hours every week (the same day and time each week is a good habit to form) to learn

something new about your eBay business or the category you sell in. Only then will you be on the road to ensuring that your business's performance is optimised. Never rest on your laurels, expecting that a business plan you put into place three years ago guarantees you the best opportunity for maximum profit.

7   Leverage your existing networks to find new products to sell on eBay. Take every opportunity to tell people what you do and remind them you are looking for more products to sell.

8   Find yourself a successful business mentor. Meet with them regularly to discuss your business openly and seek their advice on how to improve your operations; be open to criticism.

9   Attend events with other eBay and small business owners. Learning from those who have been there and done that can be the best way to fast-track your success.

10 Revisit your business plan every few months—an outdated plan can be more damaging than having no plan at all.

PART V

Running a successful eBay business (Advanced selling part II)

Questions answered in this part

Chapter 29: Managing sales and customers
- How do I keep track of my eBay sales?
- How do I find customer details?
- How can I print an invoice?
- Can I automate customer communications?
- How do I provide good service?

Chapter 30: Accepting and tracking payments
- How do I manage PayPal payments?
- How do I process other payments?
- Can I automate the unpaid item process?

(continued)

Questions answered in this part *(cont'd)*

Chapter 31: Shipping and packaging

- What shipping services do buyers expect?

- How do I sell internationally?

- What is Click and Send?

- What packaging should I use?

Chapter 32: Reporting

- What kinds of reports does eBay provide?

- How do I download PayPal reports?

Chapter 33: Troubleshooting for eBay businesses

- What is a resolution claim?

- Can I end my listing early?

- What is VeRO?

- Can I ask a buyer to review their feedback?

Chapter 29
Managing sales and customers

In previous chapters we covered branding, listing design, marketing and promotions via eBay stores, and inventory management. You have all the necessary tools for getting your eBay business live on the site, and if you've done your research and planning well, you should be seeing some of the fruits of your labour. From chapter 22, when we covered calculating profit, you'll remember that one of the highest costs any eBay business must consider is the investment of time. Once your operation is live, you need to invest in monitoring your sales and keeping customers informed of the progress of their order.

Third-party solutions such as Magento, ePages and Channel Advisor include sales and customer management tools. In many cases, you won't even need to visit eBay to keep track of your eBay business; it will all be done from the relevant program. But for most eBay businesses, the eBay-provided Selling Manager Pro solution is the best option for saving time. In part IV we covered its inventory management features, but it also includes a number of features for sales and customer management.

Selling Manager Pro—Sold view

Once you've subscribed to Selling Manager Pro, within My eBay your Sell view will automatically default to Selling Manager Pro, with its advanced functionality. If at any time you want to opt out of Selling Manager Pro, you can either unsubscribe (click My eBay at the top of any eBay page then Account then Subscriptions) or change the My eBay view back to basic by clicking View my eBay selling at the bottom of the left navigation area in My eBay.

Your primary sales management feature can be viewed by clicking Sold in the left navigation area of Selling Manager Pro in My eBay (see figure 29.1, overleaf).

Figure 29.1: the Sold view in Selling Manager Pro

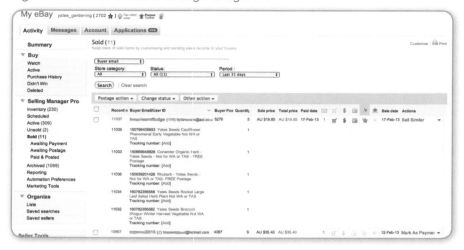

At the top of the page is the main Search drop-down that displays **Buyer email** as default. Select from the drop-down and input relevant keywords in the blank search box to search all of your sold listings by:

- *Buyer email* — your buyer's email address

- *Buyer ID* — your buyer's eBay user ID

- *Buyer name* — your buyer's first or last name

- *Sales record number* — the sales number (numerical and sequential) eBay automatically allocates to each sale

- *Item title* — your eBay listing title

- *Item ID* — the 12-digit item ID eBay allocates to each listing

- *Product name* — the product name you specified when creating your Selling Manager Pro product inventory

- *Custom label* — information you entered into the custom label field when creating your product inventory

- *Product ID* — if you entered a specific product code when creating your inventory

- *Product variation ID* — if you created multivariant listings in your product inventory and entered a specific variation code.

Beneath this, you can narrow your search of sold items by:

- *Store category* — choose from your custom list of categories if you created them in your store

- *Status* — sales awaiting payment, shipping or expedited shipment, or paid and posted

- *Period* — choose one of 15 different time periods to conduct your search.

To complete a search of sold transactions, enter the relevant information in the blank search box, choose search refinements from the drop-down then click **Search**. Corresponding results will appear in the list below.

Beneath the search options you have three drop-downs to take action on any transaction. Check the box next to your chosen transaction(s) and use one of the drop-downs for:

- *Postage action* — print postage labels or invoices, add your actual postage cost (your buyers do not see this information), add tracking number (if you're sending via a tracked shipping method)

- *Change status* — mark as payment received, posted, or paid and posted

- *Other action* — leave feedback for the buyer, send the transaction to your archived folder, download the transaction to Excel, add or edit a note for the transaction, relist the product, sell a similar item or save the product to your inventory.

The list of sold transactions appears next. From left to right, the columns display:

- *Check box* — for completing one of the actions mentioned previously

- *Record number* — as assigned sequentially by eBay every time a buyer purchases an item from you (can be clicked on to view sales record; more information on this later in this chapter)

- *Buyer details* — eBay user ID, feedback score (both can be clicked on for more information), email address, followed by item number, listing title (can be clicked on to see View item page) and link for adding tracking number

- *Custom label* — (click <u>Customise</u> at top right) then click <u>Add</u> to enter information about the transaction for your reference (buyers cannot see it)

- *Format* — (click <u>Customise</u> at top right) to add an icon for whether the listing is auction or fixed price

- *Quantity* — number of products sold

- *Sale price* — total purchase price of products sold

- *Total price* — includes postage paid if you have charged any (can be clicked on to view sales record)

- *Sale date* — the date the buyer completed checkout

- *Paid date* — the date the buyer made payment (automatically updated if PayPal has been used, but needs to be manually entered for any other payment option).

The following columns change from grey to blue when certain actions have been completed:

- *Email sent* — collates the number of emails you have sent to the buyer (can be clicked on to see a list of email types and dates)

- *Checkout* — highlights if the buyer has completed checkout (can be clicked on to view sales record)

- *Dollar sign* — highlights if the buyer has paid with PayPal or if you've manually entered a payment date and method (can be clicked on to view sales record). Note that only half the icon will turn blue if the buyer has only partially paid. If you have refunded via PayPal, an arrow will appear in front of the dollar sign.

- *Feedback left (star icon)* — highlights when you have left the buyer feedback.

- *Feedback received (star in envelope icon)* — highlights when you have received feedback from the buyer.

- *Relist status* — column appears and highlights only if you have sent the listing live again.

- *Second chance offer status* — column appears if you accept second chance offers and highlights only if you have accepted one.

- Occasionally buyers may request a total from you (once they have chosen their preferred postage method, for example). The sum equation sign will appear instead of a dollar sign if this is the case.

In the final column is a series of drop-downs to complete certain actions for each transaction:

- Mark posted

- View sales record

- Print postage labels or invoices

- Leave feedback

- Contact buyer

- Sell similar

- Relist

- Archive.

Note you can click on the heading of any column to order the transactions by this information, lowest to highest or vice versa. You can also click Customise at top right of the page to remove, add or reorder these columns. Clicking Print at top right will print transactions you have selected with the check boxes.

The sales record page

Now let's take a look at the sales record page for a more detailed overview of the transaction (see figure 29.2, overleaf).

At the top of the page you see your sales record number as automatically created by eBay. Beneath this your buyer's details appear, including user ID, email address, feedback score, address and phone number. Note to the right an empty box to enter the buyer's address; this can be done if the buyer has asked for shipment to a different address. Simply cut and paste from an email or other source and click *Move* to populate the predefined fields.

Figure 29.2: sales record

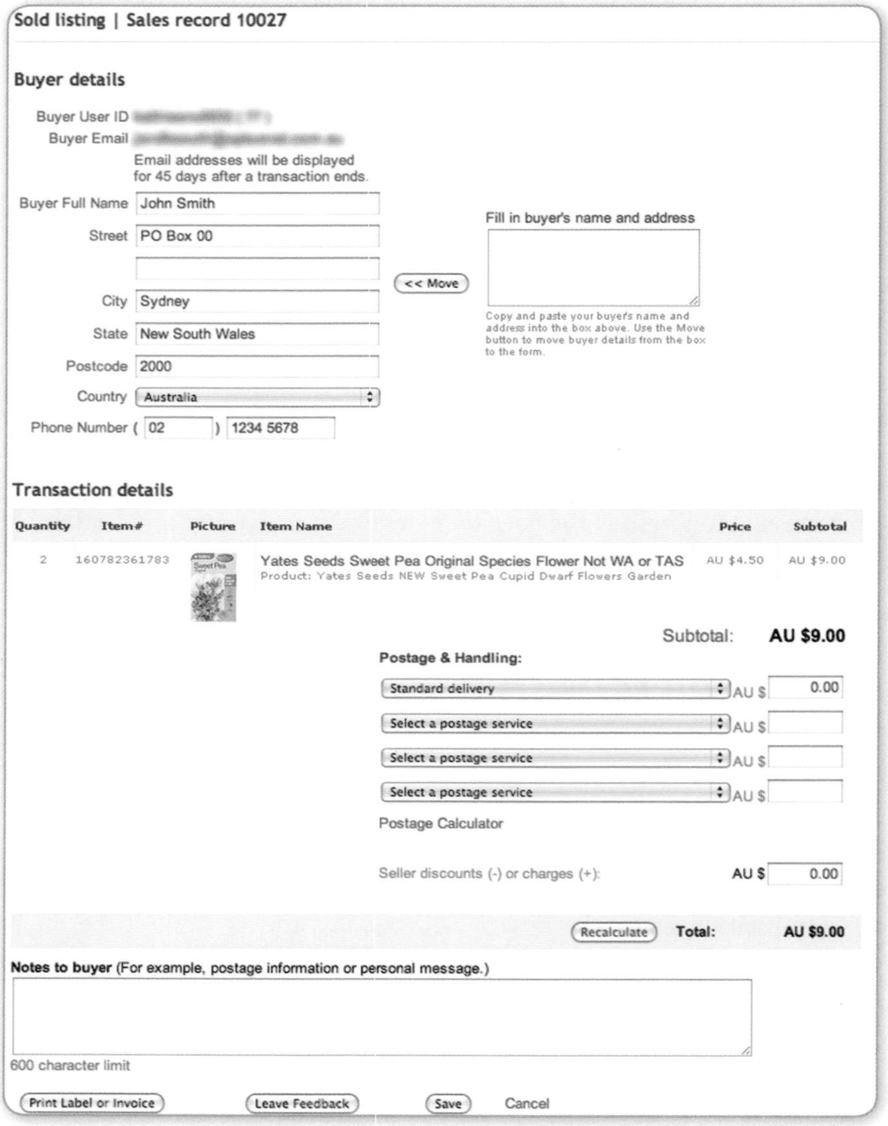

Sold listing | Sales record 10027

Buyer details

Buyer User ID ▓▓▓▓▓▓▓▓▓▓
Buyer Email ▓▓▓▓▓▓▓▓▓▓▓▓▓▓
Email addresses will be displayed
for 45 days after a transaction ends.

Buyer Full Name	John Smith
Street	PO Box 00
City	Sydney
State	New South Wales
Postcode	2000
Country	Australia
Phone Number (	02) 1234 5678

Fill in buyer's name and address

`<< Move`

Copy and paste your buyer's name and
address into the box above. Use the Move
button to move buyer details from the box
to the form.

Transaction details

Quantity	Item#	Picture	Item Name	Price	Subtotal
2	160782361783		Yates Seeds Sweet Pea Original Species Flower Not WA or TAS Product: Yates Seeds NEW Sweet Pea Cupid Dwarf Flowers Garden	AU $4.50	AU $9.00

Subtotal: **AU $9.00**

Postage & Handling:

Standard delivery AU $ 0.00

Select a postage service AU $

Select a postage service AU $

Select a postage service AU $

Postage Calculator

Seller discounts (-) or charges (+): AU $ 0.00

Recalculate Total: **AU $9.00**

Notes to buyer (For example, postage information or personal message.)

600 character limit

Print Label or Invoice   Leave Feedback   Save   Cancel

The transaction details appear next on the page:

- quantity sold

- item number

- picture of the product

- item title (can be clicked on to see the View item page)

- product name (if you have specified one when creating your inventory)

- price (individual price of each product)

- subtotal (total value of goods sold)

- postage options (generally default to your eBay rules but give you the option of adding more options, such as if your buyer pays for insurance or registered post).

The last field allows you to discount the sale if you are offering a special promotion. Click *Recalculate* to update the total of the sale. If the buyer has not completed checkout you can update this information and send the buyer an email invoice containing the new amount to be paid.

In the field at the bottom of the transaction details, enter notes to your buyer such as payment terms, returns policy or anticipated delivery times. Note that these notes will be viewable by your buyer. Three action buttons appear next:

- *Print Label or Invoice.* You can print a variety of options for your own or your buyer's records, including an invoice, sales record, packing slip (recommended for a more professional package to buyers) or address label (format labels to be printed on your computer so you don't need to write out address details for every buyer), and you can also print a copy of your store's promotional flyer if you have created one.

- *Leave feedback.* Click to leave feedback for your buyer.

- *Save.* This will save any changes you have made to the sales record.

Clicking on Cancel will cancel any changes you have made to the sales record.

Further down the page is your sale status and notes (see figure 29.3). Here the relevant sections will be highlighted once you or the buyer have taken an action:

- *Checkout*—the date the buyer completed checkout (click on the date to view the sales order details)

- *Last email sent*—the date you last sent an email to the buyer (note that some of these will be automated by eBay; click on the number in brackets to see a list of all emails sent)

- *Payment date*—the date the buyer paid you

- *Feedback sent*—if you've left feedback for your buyer

- *Postage date*—the date you marked the product as shipped

- *Feedback received*—if the buyer has left you feedback

- *Payment information*—automatically updated if the buyer paid with PayPal; otherwise enter your own date and choose the payment method the buyer used. If they paid with PayPal, click PayPal Transaction Details to be automatically directed to PayPal to view that specific transaction. This can be especially helpful if you need to locate a specific payment within a long list of recent PayPal payments or perhaps offer the buyer a refund (more information on this in the next chapter).

- *Postage information*—enter the date you shipped the item

- *Add tracking number*—click if you are using a tracked shipping method to allow buyers to trace their own parcels

- *Miscellaneous notes*—this information is not seen by buyers so you can enter your cost of goods, actual postage costs or a note about the transaction for your reference.

Action buttons are repeated at the bottom of the page.

Back in the Sold view of Selling Manager Pro, note in the left navigation area under Sold there are links for Awaiting payment, Awaiting postage and Paid & posted. Click on these to see the corresponding listings. It's a good idea to default to Awaiting postage, as these are the transactions that require your attention most urgently.

Figure 29.3: sales record, continued

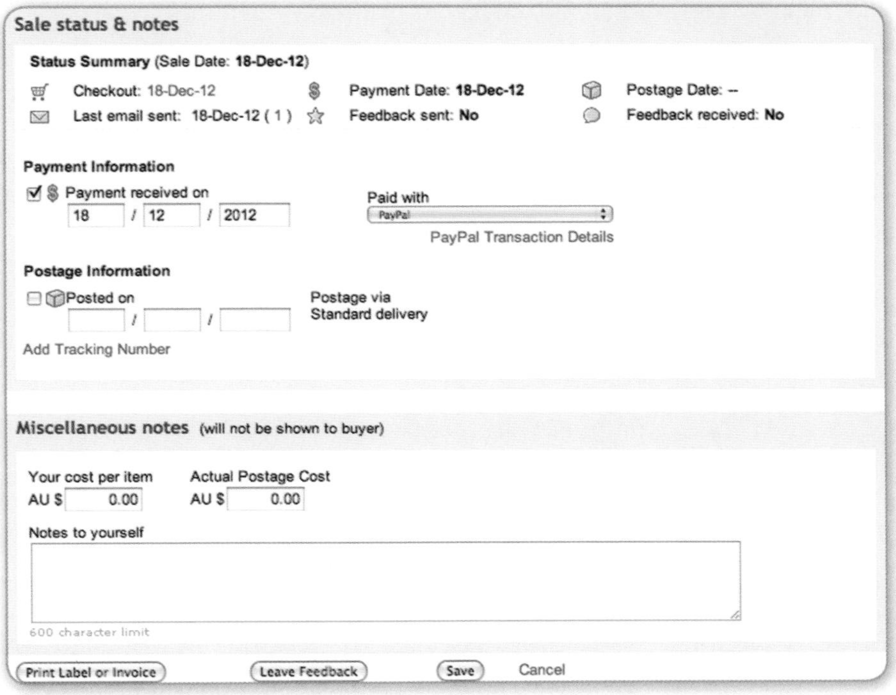

Sale status & notes

Status Summary (Sale Date: 18-Dec-12)

🛒   Checkout: 18-Dec-12 $ Payment Date: **18-Dec-12**   🎁   Postage Date: --

✉   Last email sent: 18-Dec-12 (1)   ☆   Feedback sent: **No**   〇   Feedback received: **No**

Payment Information

☑ $ Payment received on

    [18] / [12] / [2012]

Paid with

    [PayPal   ‡]

           PayPal Transaction Details

Postage Information

☐ 🎁 Posted on

    [   ] / [   ] / [   ]

Postage via
Standard delivery

Add Tracking Number

Miscellaneous notes (will not be shown to buyer)

Your cost per item   Actual Postage Cost

AU $ [0.00]   AU $ [0.00]

Notes to yourself

[   ]

600 character limit

(Print Label or Invoice)   (Leave Feedback)   (Save)   Cancel

Archived transactions

Once you've completed all of the actions against a particular transaction, it's a good idea to save it to your archive folder. Doing so will remove it from your Sold view and from your to-do list, helping you stay on top of your outstanding actions.

You can access the folder by clicking Archived in the left navigation area of Selling Manager Pro in My eBay. Here, three months of transactions are saved and you can view all of the same information you could via the Sold view. Note that some actions cannot be performed from the Archived view. One in particular you might need is to contact your buyer; to do so from the Archived view, click the sales record number, then on the sales record screen click the checkout date then Contact buyer.

It's a good idea to download your transactions each month so you can keep a permanent copy of all your sales information. We will discuss reporting further in chapter 32.

Buyer communications

If a buyer or prospective buyer contacts you, their message will appear both in your email inbox and on the *Messages* tab in My eBay. It's important to check for new messages at least daily because buyers do not like to be left hanging after they have asked a question relating to your products or your business.

You can also check your iPad and iPhone eBay apps for messages to ensure you answer them as quickly as possible. For iPhone, click the Messages link on the home screen. For iPad, click the *Navigation tab* at top left of the home screen then click Messages.

Answering emails within Messages will be a manual process, and the appearance of communications and the way to respond to them is similar to any email inbox. For easy future access, it's sensible to arrange all of your buyer communications into folders, such as those asking for refunds or returns, or those from buyers with product-related questions or compliments. Measuring communications from buyers can help you quickly identify areas for potential improvement or optimisation.

There are ways to streamline your communications with buyers and pre-empt some of the questions they may ask. Buyers should be asking questions only as a last resort—everything they need to know about your products and your business's terms of trade should be clearly stipulated within your item listing. However, some buyers will want to communicate directly with you no matter what, and while keeping customers happy is one of your main priorities, another is maintaining a healthy profit. The more time you spend answering questions, the less time you have available for streamlining other areas of your business, or sourcing new products or service providers. Your aim is to deflect buyer questions professionally before they come to your inbox.

To do so, within My eBay, click Account then click Manage communications with buyers (see figure 29.4).

Figure 29.4: managing communications with buyers

Click one of the communication types such as <u>Buyer wins auction</u> or <u>Buyer checks out</u> to view a sample communication. Click <u>Add a message</u> at bottom right to customise the communication. On the next page you will be able to enter your own text but also use tailored information links such as the buyer's name, the item number and nearly forty other options. This personalises the communication to every buyer without your having to enter his or her individual information (see figure 29.5, overleaf). In our example, you can see that every email receives a note with the customer's name in the message and it is also a good idea to include a link for the customer to email if they have any concerns or questions. You can add your own tailored links by simply leaving your cursor in your chosen place of the message field and clicking the link from the 'add to message' list on the right.

Managing sales and customers

Figure 29.5: tailoring eBay messages to your buyers

A good idea is to utilise eBay's frequently asked questions (FAQs) feature. As a bare minimum, you should also include a designated FAQs page within your store, which you can do by creating a custom page as outlined in chapter 27, but creating in-flow FAQs will mean your buyer is presented with a list of them before being able to send you a direct email. To create your own FAQs, click Edit next to 'Manage questions and answers' on the 'Manage communications with buyers' screen. On the next screen, check the 'Show Q&A' box (see figure 29.6). Click one of the subject areas such as Item details then Add more questions to add questions and answers within that topic. If you've already created questions and need to remove or edit them, click on the question to view more information, then click Edit or Remove. Click Submit to create your FAQs. My FAQs save me considerable time and energy answering the same questions from different buyers—they are a must-have for profitable eBay businesses.

Figure 29.6: managing your Q&A for buyers

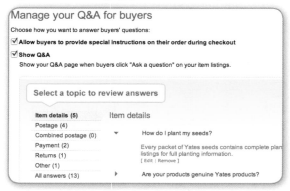

Store subscribers can add their logo and branding to many of their communications to buyers, as covered in chapter 27, by clicking on <u>Logos and branding</u> within the Manage my store page of My eBay.

> ### Get customer communication right
>
> Every communication with a buyer or prospective customer is an opportunity to create a loyal customer for life. Always treat your customers with respect and professionalism, even if the question they are asking is clearly answered in your listings or you think the question is less than intelligent. Remember that being an eBay business is about providing the best service, and you never know which of your customers might turn out to be your most loyal, and most profitable. Always check your spelling and use a tone that is friendly but to the point. Over-communication can be as much of a customer turn-off as never answering a question at all.

Customer service dos and don'ts

Running an eBay business is like running any other business where customers are involved: you should create a set of minimum service standards that you and your staff can adhere to. In fact, because on eBay buyers are purchasing a product they have never seen from someone they have never met, they may have higher service expectations than, say, within a retail store. You need to take customer service seriously, and if you think starting an eBay business is a way of avoiding customers simply because there's little face-to-face communication, then you won't be profitable in the long run. For many of us, customer service may be a new skill we need to learn. The good and the bad news is that there's no one single answer when it comes to what is right and what is wrong. You can't just learn from a checklist but will need to tailor your level of service to the products you sell and the kinds of buyers those products attract.

Table 29.1 (overleaf) sets out some general guidelines to consider as a starting point in creating your own service standards for your eBay business. Add to these over time or remove the ones that don't apply, and remember to continually shop from your competitors online, on eBay, locally and internationally, and from physical stores, so you can assess your own service objectively and seek to become the best example within your category.

Managing sales and customers

Table 29.1: guidelines for good customer communication

Do	Don't
Take a personal interest in how your customers are being treated	Give customer service responsibility to someone who does not like customers or is not a great communicator
Take the time to create standard answers and responses to commonly asked questions — it will save you a lot of time in the future	Over-communicate — too many words can be distracting and create mistrust
Read every communication to buyers twice, checking for spelling errors and possible misunderstandings, and removing all ambiguity	Ignore a customer — ever
Respond as soon as you are capable — aim for a maximum response time of 24 hours, but even this may be considered slow by online customers	Think your customers are stupid or annoying. You've got them wrong and you can learn from them and provide better information and service
Keep track of your communications — collect common topics so you can address your business operations accordingly	Communicate with customers if you're in a bad mood. Try to wait for it to pass — customers will think you don't want their business
Offer a variety of contact methods — some buyers respond much better to a phone call than to a written communication	Send your customers elsewhere for answers — find the answer for them
Think of every communication as a chance to make more profit — and act accordingly	Hold your customers to eBay feedback ransom. If they leave positive comments, great. If they don't, do not harass them. Try to learn from negative comments rather than insist that your customers have got it wrong.

Other customer service options

You may find that your eBay business attracts more customers than you had targeted or planned for. While Selling Manager Pro and other eBay features might be sufficient for your needs to begin with, in the future you may find that customer communications are taking too much of a toll on your staff and costing you too much time and energy. As covered in chapter 25, third-party tools such as Magento also feature customer service tools to help streamline your operations. An internet search will show you other options. If you get really big, you could consider outsourcing your customer service operations.

Whatever you decide, keep in mind the amount of time you invest in communications, and continually strive to streamline this component of your eBay business. Before committing to a new software system or service, make sure you have fully investigated all of the product's features and completely understand any ongoing commitments you might have. Training staff or agents in customer service will inevitably mean a period of readjustment for your customers, so plan well to keep disruptions to a minimum.

If ever you're unsure of the best direction to take your service efforts, reach out to your customers to better understand what their expectations are. You can do this directly by including a reply-paid survey in the packages you send to your buyers, or carefully review the feedback and emails you receive from them. Free survey software can also be found online, and you can consider incorporating a link to your customer satisfaction survey at the bottom of all your buyer communications.

Leave feedback

Being a professional business on eBay means you will leave feedback for your buyers as soon as they have paid for their product. This is the only requirement of the buyer—that they pay. Some sellers refuse to leave feedback for buyers until they have received positive feedback, but this only contributes to a general feeling of mistrust. Leaving positive, professional and branded feedback instils confidence in your buyers and sets the tone for the rest of the transaction, up to and including their leaving feedback for you.

Not all buyers leave feedback. It is optional, and while your business would benefit from having as much positive feedback as possible, it's not worth annoying your customers by begging them to leave you feedback or DSRs.

You can automate the feedback you leave for your buyers so you never need to worry about doing it manually. Click My eBay at the top of any eBay page and then click Automation preferences in the left navigation area under Selling Manager Pro. Check the box next to the heading 'Automatically leave the following positive feedback' and click Edit stored comments to create your own. Check 'Buyer has paid for this item' then click *Apply*.

Leave positive feedback

Create up to 10 different positive, professional and branded stored feedback comments. Always use your store name or user ID within the comment. Consider phrases such as 'Thank you for buying from [enter your details]', 'Thanks from [enter your ID], we hope to see you again' or 'Thank you for choosing [enter your ID] for your [enter your main product category] purchase'—for example, 'Thank you for choosing Yates Gardening as your seeds supplier on eBay'. You're using this opportunity to extend your on-eBay brand awareness. To any buyer viewing feedback left for other members.

Block problem buyers

Of course, it is *your* eBay business and you are entitled to restrict certain people from entering your virtual premises. Perhaps you had a disagreement in the past or feel that a buyer's behaviour towards you or your staff was unacceptable. You can block certain types of, or individual, buyers from purchasing your products. To do so, click Selling Manager Pro in the left navigation area of My eBay to be taken to your summary. Scroll down the page to find the 'Favourite links' heading then click Block bidders. Here you'll be able to block specific user IDs from purchasing your products on eBay.

You can also set minimum buyer requirements across all of your listings, such as for those who have received unpaid item strikes, have eBay policy violations or have a negative feedback score. To set your requirements across all your listings, click *Account* in My eBay then click Site preferences then Show next to Buyer requirements, then click Edit.

Chapter 30
Accepting and tracking payments

We've covered the various payment methods previously, in parts III and IV, but in this chapter we'll explore the most efficient ways of accepting and tracking payments for your eBay business.

PayPal

Because it's owned by eBay, PayPal has been very well integrated into the transactional functions within eBay. As outlined previously, when one of your buyers pays using PayPal, eBay automatically syncs that payment with your Selling Manager views so you don't need to check your PayPal account for paid status. Coupled with the ability to click on links from the sales record directly to the corresponding PayPal record, this means that the more buyers who use PayPal, the less time and energy you spend collating payments with the correct buyer.

Let's take a moment to look at the PayPal website to highlight a few additional features of this payment mechanism. Log into your PayPal account to view your account overview (see figure 30.1, overleaf).

At the top of the page under *My Account* are links to various functions on the PayPal site:

- Overview. The default view shows a list of all recent transactions.

- Add funds. This allows you to withdraw money from your bank account and deposit into PayPal (if you have linked one to your PayPal account).

- Withdraw. This allows you to withdraw a positive balance from your PayPal account into your linked bank account.

- History. View and search across all of your PayPal transactions in the past. On the history screen, click Find a transaction to search by 12 different pieces of information, including buyer email and names.

Figure 30.1: PayPal account summary

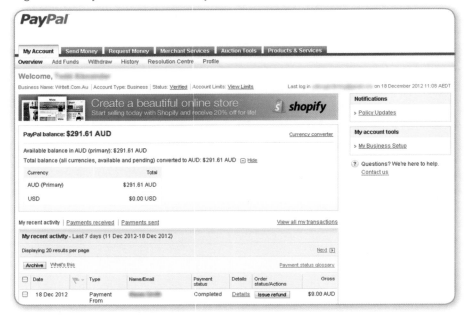

- <u>Resolution centre</u>. If a buyer has lodged a PayPal Buyer Protection claim or you have made a claim for Seller Protection (more on that later in this chapter), the details plus any outstanding actions will be listed here.

- <u>Profile</u>. Add information or edit your PayPal account information here. Note this is also where your linked bank and credit card information can be updated.

Beneath this you will see your current PayPal balance. If you accept payments in multiple currencies, a list of separate currencies will be shown. Further down the page are links to <u>Payments received</u>, <u>Payments sent</u> and <u>View all transactions</u>. Clicking on one of these will show you the relevant listings beneath.

In the transactions list you will see the date, whether the payment has been received or sent, the name of the buyer (or seller if you've paid someone), the payment status, a link to <u>Details</u> (takes you to view the transaction details), a button to *Issue refund* (you have up to 60 days to issue a refund), and the gross amount paid by the buyer. From the transaction details page you can see all of the information relating to the sale, including the buyer's name, email address and physical address; and you can print a PayPal packing slip and add tracking information on this page. You can also view the PayPal fees paid for this transaction.

PayPal offers a lot more functionality for businesses outside of eBay, and it's well worth exploring its website to see which of these you can utilise in your own business. Options include invoicing, mobile payments and incorporating a shopping cart into your website. For more information click the **Merchant services** tab once you are logged into PayPal.

If you'd like PayPal to be the payment option you prefer buyers to use, you can specify this within your listings. To apply to all listings click My eBay at the top of any page, then click Account then Site preferences. Next to the heading 'Payment from buyers' click Show then Edit to update your options.

Bank deposit

Accepting deposits directly into your bank account is the cheapest way to receive funds for your eBay sales in terms of fees per transaction, but it can be one of the most costly in terms of time investment and protection. Bank deposit is not integrated into eBay, so a buyer has to pay by manually logging into their internet banking or walking into a branch of the bank used by your business. As a result, there is no way to automatically sync a payment with a specific eBay transaction. In my business I actively encourage and prefer PayPal because I do not want to waste time tracking transactions.

Normally the bank deposit sequence is as follows. The buyer completes checkout and gets your bank details during the process or contacts you to email them your bank details. The buyer pays using bank transfer and usually tells you when they have paid. If you have not heard from the buyer you will need to check your bank account every day for deposited funds. You go to your internet banking and check for deposited funds. Once located, you check that the amount is correct and that the buyer has included a reference. Some buyers do not include a reference so it's impossible to know who deposited the funds. When you sell multiple items of the same value, it can be very difficult to trace payments to individual buyers. Once you've connected the deposited funds with the correct buyer, you then log into eBay to mark the transaction as paid, and specify which payment method was used.

The entire process can take anywhere from three to seven days, depending on the financial institutions used. Bank deposit certainly has its place for infrequent sales but think carefully whether this is a time commitment you are willing to make. Most eBay buyers have a PayPal account and can use this option instead of paying via a bank account.

It's also difficult to download reports from your internet banking that specifically relate to eBay transactions, whereas most other payment mechanisms provide reporting functionality. Finally, neither buyer nor seller is covered in the event that something goes wrong, so if you do need to provide a refund to the buyer you will need to contact them again to get their bank details so you can then process another bank transfer to refund their original amount!

If you do choose to accept bank deposit, however, it's best to utilise Bank deposit express, which makes it faster for buyers to pay as your bank details will appear clearly within checkout. To apply Bank deposit express to all of your listings, click My eBay at the top of any page then click Account then Site preferences. Next to the heading 'Payment from buyers' click Show then Edit to update your options.

Paymate

Paymate provides similar functionality to PayPal and is also integrated into some components of the eBay website. To accept Paymate payments you need to:

• register with Paymate

• link your eBay and Paymate IDs via the Paymate website, where you'll then be directed to eBay to grant access for Paymate Express payments

• offer Paymate as a payment option on your eBay listings.

Buyers will then be able to checkout without signing up for Paymate, simply by entering their credit card information on a secure Paymate payment page. The funds are automatically deposited into your nominated bank account.

Merchant credit card

Merchant credit-card processing is integrated into eBay's checkout if you utilise either Cybersource or Payflow (the PayPal owned gateway). However, if you're not using either of these, then you will need to communicate directly with your buyers to get their credit card information, and enter it manually into your processor.

To incorporate credit-card processing into eBay checkout, click My eBay at the top of any page then click the **Account** tab then Site preferences then Payment from buyers then Edit.

> **Tip**
>
> ## On credit card security
>
> If manually processing your customer's credit card details, you are legally bound to comply with PCI (Payment Card Industry) regulations. These relate to how you store and communicate customers' financial information. An internet search or your financial provider will be able to provide more information.

Other payment methods

Refer to part III of this book for other payment methods such as bank cheques and money orders and how to process them. Most eBay businesses do not accept these more archaic payment options as the time delay for funds to clear can cause buyer frustration. Remember that it is also against eBay policy to accept online money transfers from providers such as Western Union and MoneyGram.

Automate unpaid items

Sometimes a buyer completes checkout but then doesn't follow through with payment. This can be frustrating to your business because the product will no longer be available to other buyers and eBay will charge you a final value fee unless you lodge an unpaid item claim. It's advisable always to lodge an unpaid item claim because not only can it result in your receiving a refund on eBay fees, but it also marks that buyer in the eBay system as an nonpaying buyer, which can lead to restrictions on their account.

You can establish an automated Unpaid item assistant that will do this for you without your having to make any special arrangements with eBay or the

Accepting and tracking payments

buyer. To launch the assistant, click **Account** in My eBay then click <u>Show</u> next to the 'Unpaid item assistant' heading. Click <u>Edit</u> to choose how quickly you would like eBay to open an unpaid item on your behalf, whether you would like to receive email notifications and if there are any buyers you would like to exclude from the automated claim process.

As covered in part III, you could also make a second chance offer on the listing, giving another interested buyer the option of purchasing it and saving you the effort of relisting the item if it's a single-quantity product.

Chapter 31
Shipping and packaging

You could have the nicest looking eBay business in the world, with fantastic products that are very popular with buyers, but unless you get those products safely into the hands of your buyers you'll be losing customers on a regular basis. More than this, however, the way you ship and package your products is the final part of the buyer experience, and one where you can separate your business from that of competitors. Packing items professionally and with your branding helps keep buyers happy. As this may be your final communication with the buyer, it is your last chance to make them loyal, frequent shoppers.

One of eBay's largest sellers tells me that the business he is in is logistics. In other words, he sees his primary business function as getting a product from his supplier into the hands of his customer. If he does that, and does it well, then his business will be successful. Choosing the right shipping partner (or partners) is critical for both your profit margin and the overall success of your business. After all, if you're not delivering the products yourself, you're relying on a third party to complete the final, and most important, part of the transaction.

What buyers expect

Here are some of the things you should consider when choosing shipping and packaging options. Depending on the products you sell, some or all of the options may be appropriate for your eBay business.

Free shipping

As business owners, we all know there is no such thing as free shipping. What buyers are increasingly demanding, however, is that the cost of shipping not be added onto the total cost of the sale during checkout. Some sellers are able to absorb the shipping cost within their item price so the buyer thinks they are paying no extra for this service. You'd be surprised how positively buyers embrace the idea of 'free' delivery. I've spoken to a range of eBay sellers and encouraged all of them to experiment with their item/shipping price. Some have found that selling at a higher price while offering 'free shipping' attracts more buyers than selling at a lower price and adding a shipping cost on top. Experiment with your buyers to gauge which option attracts the most interest.

Express shipping

Professional sellers also ensure they offer buyers an express shipping option, even if this comes at an additional cost to buyers. Some are willing to pay for it to ensure they get the product before a set deadline.

Insurance/registered post

Sellers cannot make it mandatory for buyers to take out postage insurance and while it can be offered for buyers, you cannot ask them for extra payment for this service. One option for business risk management is to take out blanket transit insurance (often called Marine Insurance) to cover you for everything shipped or to only use insured postal services. Some couriers will offer insurance on each consignment, either as a blanket policy, or on an individual item opt-in basis. A shipping aggregator such as Temando (www.temando.com) can facilitate this insurance, which can be opted-in by the sender at the time of booking.

Courier

Depending on the size of your items, you may need to offer courier services. eBay has been working on a solution that will allow businesses to incorporate courier costs to different regions in Australia — click Community at the top of any eBay page then click News for the latest developments. You may want to investigate software add-ons to include in your listings so buyers can enter their own postcode and view the courier costs.

Tracked shipping

Using tracked shipping methods will allow buyers to trace their own products during the delivery process. This will reduce the time you need to spend responding to customers chasing you for their products. If using tracked methods, choose an online service so buyers can trace their delivery with a few clicks of the mouse rather than having to sit on the phone to your shipping provider for extended periods. Remember also that tracked shipping is required for you to be eligible for PayPal Seller Protection.

Other considerations

Other matters of importance to buyers in relation to shipping and handling include:

• appropriate packaging (take the time to investigate the right packaging for each of your products; outlined in more detail later in the chapter)

• handling time of less than two days (preferably same day or next day)

• communications from you when milestones have been met (payment received, item shipped and so on)

• a returns policy in the event that the product delivered is faulty or not suitable for the buyer's needs.

Sell internationally

Before we cover the various shipping and packing options, consider listing internationally with eBay. You will be able to open your products for potential sale to tens of millions of active buyers across the globe, and if you have products that are harder to find in overseas markets you may stumble across a ready-made extension for your business. Some of eBay's largest and most entrepreneurial sellers have embraced this functionality as a way to vastly increase the number of buyers for their products.

There are no additional eBay fees to open your products for sale on international eBay sites — you can do so simply by adding an international postage option within your listing. Adding an international postage option will mean buyers in the countries you choose to send to will be able to purchase your products (usually via PayPal) and pay you in Australian currency (the price will automatically be converted to their local currency for easy calculation).

You may also wish to consider selling directly on an overseas eBay site — that is, log directly into the UK or US site, for example, and complete the listing process there. This will display the product in the local currency and the buyers will pay you in their own currency (usually via PayPal, which will then convert the payment back into Australian dollars and place it in your account).

If you list directly on an eBay site outside Australia, your listings will be subject to the fees charged by the local site. Refer to your chosen site for an outline of all listing fees.

Handling

Most buyers expect handling time (that is, the time between them paying for an item and you giving it to a shipping service for delivery) to be less than two days. Ideal business practice to adopt is same-day or one-day handling time. You want to get the product to your buyers as soon as is practical, so any delays that can be avoided must be. Refer also to chapter 26 for the impact of handling time on your search position within Best match.

Wherever possible, avoid charging buyers extra for handling. The internal costs (labour, machinery and so on) of getting the product from your business to the shipping provider is not something buyers like to pay extra for. Charging for handling may affect the number of buyers you attract.

Communicate with buyers

As covered in chapter 25, by using Selling Manager Pro you elect when and what types of communications buyers receive. As a bare minimum, you should communicate when you have shipped the item and, if applicable, give buyers details for how they can track the product and when to expect it. Setting clear buyer expectations is part of the challenge of providing good customer service. You want your buyers to be informed but not anxious if your suggested timelines are not being met. Give them a reasonable range of time within which to expect delivery, and provide your contact details on every communication so buyers can reach out to you if they have questions or concerns.

Using Selling Manager, mark a product as shipped only once it has left your premises. Doing so as you pick or pack the product may create a false expectation in your buyer's mind that they will receive it sooner. If you live in a rural area, it's worth spelling out to your buyers that mail can take longer to reach some destinations. Clearly specify this in your listings and when providing an estimate of when the product will arrive.

Include a call to action with every package you send. This could be your store promotional flyer (as covered in chapter 27), a product catalogue, suggestions for product use or even something as simple as a printed postcard. I recently received a package from an eBay business in the US in which the business owner had included a card (see figure 31.1) that not only said thank you and to contact him should I have any questions or concerns, but also offered me a 10 per cent discount off my next purchase from his eBay store. It was a simple idea but it worked — I went back to his store the next week and purchased again. He kindly gave me permission to reproduce the sample postcard for this book. You can emulate his professionalism. Note the URL for his store at the top of the card, the clear offer of a discount (and how simple it sounds to claim), his email address for contacting with questions, and a reminder that he'd left me positive feedback and, without being pushy about it, he would appreciate the same!

Figure 31.1: example thank-you note and discount offer

Thank you for your business!
http://stores.ebay.com/Georges-Toy-Chest

I hope you are 100% satisfied with your item! If there are any problems, please contact me immediately, before leaving feedback, at
GeorgesToyChest@gmail.com.
I will work to ensure your satisfaction!

If you are happy with your item, please leave positive feedback and 5-star DSR ratings. I have already left you positive feedback!

Thank you again and I hope to do business with you in the future!

All the best, *George*

A special discount for you!

To thank you for your business, on your next purchase from either my eBay auctions or my eBay store, I will send you a 10% refund of the total purchase price. Just send me an email and mention the code "POSTCARD10". Once I receive your payment, I will refund 10% of the purchase price via PayPal. Only one promo code may be used per order per customer.

Australia Post

For most eBay businesses, Australia Post provides all or most of their shipping services. Becoming friendly with your local Australia Post staff is critical to ensuring you make the most of the services they have on offer. Don't assume that an off-the-shelf option is the best and most cost-effective solution for your business. Visit the Australia Post website (www.auspost.com.au) and type 'eBay' into the search box to see multiple pages relating to how Australia Post can help streamline your eBay business. Over the years, eBay and Australia Post have worked together closely to offer more delivery options, some at reduced prices.

Among the most important features on Australia Post is its Click and Send functionality. Click and Send allows you to print shipping labels and pay for shipping without having to leave your office. It is integrated into eBay's postage-centre back end, meaning each sold product can have a separate label automatically printed. You attach the paid label to your product and place it in an Australia Post box. It's that simple. You can choose from a variety of delivery options including:

- Parcel Post Plus

- Express Post

- Express Post Platinum

- International options, including Pack & Track, Express Post, Express Courier and Registered Post.

Click and Send provides a range of buyer benefits, including offering specific delivery days or time windows, a choice to collect their purchase from Australia Post or one of its new Parcel Locker outlets, tracking capabilities and the ability to redirect a package using Australia Post's My Deliveries online tool. You can sync your eBay and Click and Send accounts easily by following the prompts at the Australia Post website. For more information visit http://v2.clickandsend.com.au.

Another development between the two companies are the eBay/Australia Post co-branded prepaid satchels and boxes. You can purchase your packages in bulk for less than you would pay at an Australia Post retail outlet. The satchels and boxes come in a range of sizes and prices to suit most small to medium-sized products, from 500 g to 3 kg.

Spend some time searching the Australia Post website thoroughly to review its complete range of business services, including post, courier and other logistics solutions. Speak to your local Australia Post staff about pick-up options too. If your business is large enough it may qualify for complementary pick-up so you don't have to take the packages to Australia Post yourself (saving you time, fuel, and wear and tear on your vehicle). Larger businesses may also qualify for an Australia Post account manager, who can visit your business to provide tailored shipping and logistics solutions for your needs.

Couriers

If you're using couriers for your eBay business, ensure you collect a range of quotes from multiple suppliers. It's important to note that each courier charges different amounts for different regions in Australia, so one courier may not be able to provide the best service for all of your customers and it might be more profitable to use a number of different couriers.

Where possible, use a courier that provides online tracking functionality so your buyers can easily trace the progress of their package without needing to contact you or the courier company. Some couriers require signature on delivery, so communicate this clearly to your buyers and make sure you also have the buyer's phone number (displayed within the sold listing record in Selling Manager Pro) as most couriers will insist on a phone number before delivering.

It's a good idea to send some products to your friends or family using different couriers and to ask them about their experiences with each. Remember that the courier driver may be your buyer's final experience with your business and it's often this last impression that lingers longest.

An internet search will show scores of options. Look for couriers who highlight servicing eBay businesses as a competitive advantage. They are most likely to understand your requirements and help you integrate their services with your own business operations to minimise overheads and maximise your profit.

View your courier service provider(s) as business partners, and where possible elevate your business in their consciousness so you're not just another number or a voice on the end of the phone. A great courier company will offer you account management and tailored solutions rather than forcing you into a 'one size fits all' model. Even when you find the company that's right for you, it's sensible to reassess your options every year, as rates and services change and reducing your shipping costs is one of the most effective ways of increasing your profit.

You could also consider utilising the services of shipping aggregators such as www.temando.com, www.readytoship.com.au and www.jedcart.com, which provide access to multiple couriers to compare real-time quotes without needing to open individual accounts with each courier.

Shipping and packaging

Local pick-up

It's entirely up to you whether you would like to offer a local pick-up option for buyers to come to your place of business to collect the product themselves. Never charge for local pick-up handling, and ensure you give buyers a clear outline of your business operating hours or hours for collection. Define a safe and clearly designated area for pick-ups and place products neatly in the area when a pick-up is expected. The last thing a buyer wants to do is wait around for you or your staff to search for something or scoot about your warehouse on a forklift to retrieve their dusty product from a distant corner.

Clearly label the pick-up area from your driveway so buyers know where to park their vehicle. Ensure there are no hazards or obstructions near where customers will be driving or walking. Consider your business insurance options if regular pick-ups will be occurring — you may need additional liability insurance to protect your business from damage caused to your customers or their vehicles.

Whoever deals with customer pick-ups needs to be courteous, professional and an extension of your brand. Sometimes this isn't your forklift driver or truck driver. It should be someone who understands the basics of customer service and knows how to impress your buyers enough that they find the overall experience a positive one.

If you operate your eBay business from home, pick-ups should be available from a clean and tidy area of your house or property.

Packaging

Buyers hate having to waste a lot of time and effort trying to get into the package you send. While it's important that you package the product well, you don't need to go overboard with sticky tape so every visible join is taped over multiple times. The frustration this can cause can actually prompt buyers to be less careful when opening your safe-like package and as a result can lead to unintentional damage during the opening process. Be secure, but don't cause an inconvenience.

Fragile items should always be carefully packaged with appropriate insulation such as foam, shredded paper or bubble wrap. Buy your packaging materials in bulk (consider looking for them on eBay) and don't skimp when it comes to breakable products. Consider environmentally friendly options if you need to include a lot of material to keep your products safe.

Recycling packages to send your products is great for the environment but doesn't always create the best impression on buyers. I've even come across sellers who have used garbage bags to package their products. This is where the expression 'think like a retailer' comes into play again: if you package your products in the way a retailer would, you'll be exceeding your buyers' expectations. While retailers have branded bags and professional customer service staff to hand or deliver them neatly to customers, you have to rely on your shipping service to get the products to your buyers and it's that first impression that often sums up your entire brand for the buyer. Using an old cauliflower box to send your products isn't thinking like a retailer (unless you're selling cauliflowers, that is!). If your product is new, your packaging should be too. Look for environmentally friendly new packaging products rather than trying to use up any old thing you have lying around the house or office.

The best eBay businesses have packaging that is branded with their logo or colours and design. They invest in packaging that is unique to their business and has been tailor-made for the products they sell. Shoving your products inside an Australia Post envelope is doing nothing for your brand's reputation or the safe delivery of your products. While it's an added expense, and it's difficult to measure the precise impact on sales, consider printing bespoke packaging for your online business. Remember that everything you send should clearly state your business name and the URL of your eBay store.

Returns

In Australia it has become the professional standard that buyers can return products they have purchased online. Some businesses offer the minimum returns window (seven days, which is not really practical given shipping times), while others take it to the other extreme and offer a 365-day return window. Some Australian businesses are legally obliged to offer returns—check with your business adviser or lawyer to see if this applies to your operation. Whether a business wants to or not, increasing buyer demand requires all businesses to offer a returns window if it wants to attract buyers, and repeat business.

Depending on the products you sell, specify a returns window of 30 days or more. This gives buyers ample time to receive, open and test the product. Some businesses use their returns policy as a point of difference—'Buy three different sizes from us and simply return the ones that do not fit'—as this attracts more buyers than having no clear returns policy at all. This is particularly beneficial if you're selling clothing or other practical, tangible products. Imagine the peace of mind you'd be affording your buyers if you actively encouraged them to purchase a range of colours, styles or sizes and return those they found unsuitable. After all, you'll have no way of knowing how many buyers look at your products, love the look of your eBay business but are just hesitant that the product might not be ideal for their purpose. Most businesses, *regardless of their returns policy*, should budget for a set percentage number of returns each year. Those offering 365-day windows generally see no substantial rise in the number of returns.

The other component of offering returns is the question of who pays for the shipping from the buyer back to your business. Highly competitive businesses pay for this out of their own pocket, but it is yet to be something buyers generally demand. When you consider what retail shoppers pay to get themselves from home to the store (such as fuel or public transport costs, and parking fees), buyers generally understand that a return will involve some cost or inconvenience. Having said that, supplying a reply-paid label in every package you send is the ultimate in buyer comfort. You can only gauge its impact by conducting small tests to see what this does to (a) your returns levels and (b) your percentage of repeat buyers.

Competitive awareness

Whatever you choose for your shipping and packaging solutions, it's useful to continue shopping regularly from your competitors. They may be faster to adapt to new technologies or methods, and you can easily find that your well-researched solutions have quickly fallen out of favour with your buyers. Every solution you choose is an opportunity to exceed the services offered by anyone else selling products in your category—whether eBay businesses, websites outside eBay, local or international operations, or traditional bricks-and-mortar stores. The challenge is to provide the best, but to do so at a manageable cost that preserves your profit margin.

Chapter 32
Reporting

Another key to successful, profitable business is to conduct regular and thorough reports on various aspects of your operation. eBay provides a number of reporting mechanisms to allow you to measure, track and improve your business's progress.

Selling Manager Pro

Click Reporting in the left navigation area under Selling Manager Pro in My eBay. Here you will be able to download reports going back 18 months into an Excel format for you to save on your computer or print to paper. The reports include a daily breakdown of sales, quantity sold and cost of sales (if you entered cost into your product inventory). You can also choose to report on each of your store categories.

Stores reporting

When you subscribe to an eBay store, you can access two different types of reports. These links can be found under the 'Reports' heading in the left navigation area of Manage my store.

Traffic reports are provided by an external party called Omniture (see figure 32.1, overleaf). Once you have activated your reports (you need to do this every 90 days if you have not used them in the interim), you will be able to view your store's:

• *number of page views* — every time a visitor views any of your listings or store pages (data provided is month to date, four weeks prior and previous year)

• *visits* — the number of single buyers browsing your store pages for 30 minutes or more without a break

- *storefront homepage*—how many times your homepage was viewed (your homepage is the first page customers see when they click on your store)

- *most popular pages*—a list of your most viewed pages.

Click <u>View full report</u> from your summary page to see more detailed information relating to each. On this page you can see:

- daily data for each of the reports

- links to download the report in various formats (at the top of the page).

Figure 32.1: store traffic reports provided by Omniture

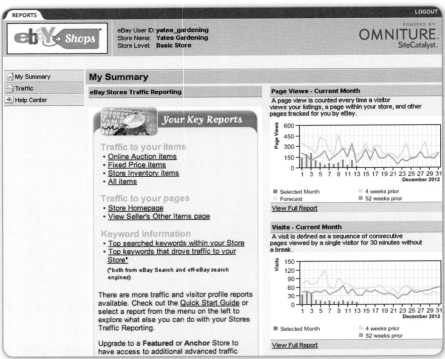

You'll also find the following links:

- Referring domains shows you which websites directed traffic to your store.

- Search engines shows you how those directed from outside eBay found your store.

- Search keywords shows you which keywords buyers entered most frequently to find your store.

- Most popular listings shows you which of your products have received the most page views from within your store.

- Store search terms shows you which terms have been entered into your store's search box most frequently.

Sales reports are the other kind of report accessed by the link under the 'Reports' heading in the left navigation area of Manage my store. From within sales reports you will see a summary of your sales (dollar value, number of sold items and average selling price), eBay and PayPal fees paid, and unpaid items over the past weeks or month trended over time. At the bottom of your sales report, you will also see information such as total number of buyers, total unique buyers and percentage of repeat buyers. This is a lead indicator of whether your marketing to attract more repeat customers is working. Other reports include sales by category and sales by format, including ending day, ending time and duration. Click Archived reports to see all of your data dating back 24 months. Click Download at top right of any report to save it to your computer.

Sales reports are the best summary of your top-level eBay activity and will help with accounting, identifying trends and reporting for tax purposes.

Tip

Use Listing analytics

Listing analytics help you gauge how your listings are performing in eBay search, and also allows you to see how you're performing compared to the top 5 listings. To access Listing analytics, click My eBay at the top of any page then click Analytics.

PayPal reporting

If you're using PayPal as a payment method, you can download detailed reports directly from the PayPal website. To access reporting, click **My account** then History then Download my history. You can download a variety of reports for specific time periods in multiple formats, including Excel and formats to suit Quick and Quickbooks business accounting software.

Other reporting

While not automated via eBay, it's advisable to conduct a regular audit of all your business's outgoings. Each month you should be able to easily calculate all of the costs associated with running your business. Keep watch for any unusual increase in costs and, where possible, negotiate with your suppliers to ensure you are receiving the best price and solution for your business. Remember that sometimes paying more money for a more advanced solution may help you reduce other overheads and result in higher profit at the end of the month or in years to come.

You might consider using small business accounting software to help you keep track of your income and outgoing costs, and prepare necessary documentation for your accountant or tax return. Some solutions, such as MYOB (www.myob.com.au), include eBay integration, but conduct an internet search to view more options.

Keep transaction records

As eBay transaction records only remain accessible for 90 days you will need to record the transaction information in your own bookkeeping system regularly. This will help ensure you don't lose critical information needed for completing tax returns and business financial reporting.

Chapter 33
Troubleshooting for eBay businesses

Running an eBay business can often be a full-time job. As you increase the number of products you sell and your customer base, you also increase the probability of encountering some common problems. Don't panic! These issues are all par for the course and there are simple solutions in place to help you solve them and get on with running your profitable business.

My buyer lodged a resolution claim against me

Buyers may lodge resolution claims against you with either eBay or PayPal. Most buyers are diligent in contacting you first to resolve problems, but a few are less aware of the protocol and will go straight to one or other company. In this case, always react calmly and assume the buyer did not know how to contact you or was unaware of the convention to do so. All of your communications with the buyer should be courteous and professional, even if you feel what they are asking is unreasonable.

My attitude with buyer complaints is that investing in solving today's problem could well result in increased sales tomorrow (either from that buyer or through positive word of mouth). You can access the resolution centre by clicking My eBay at the top of any eBay page, then click Account then Resolution centre.

I need to end a listing early

You may unexpectedly run out of stock of a product or have miscalculated the available quantity, or perhaps you have another reason for wanting to end a listing early. You can end fixed price listings any time. As covered in part IV, click Active under Selling Manager Pro in My eBay, check the box next to the relevant listing then click *End*.

There are restrictions on when you can end an auction listing. For example, you cannot end an auction when there is less than 12 hours remaining and you have received a bid. To read the full list of rules for ending an auction listing, click Customer support at the top of any eBay page then type 'end auction' into the search box and click *Search*. Click Ending your listing early to see the relevant information.

Another listing has infringed my copyright

If you suspect another seller has used your copyright images or text, you can alert eBay to the issue and they will investigate. Where there is clear infringement of copyright, action may be taken against the other seller. To report a possible infringement, click Report item on the relevant View item page and follow the prompts.

I've broken an eBay rule

As an eBay user who has read and agreed to the terms and conditions of the user agreement, it's your responsibility to understand, and follow, eBay's rules, particularly those for selling. From time to time you may receive notice from eBay that you have contravened one of their selling rules. If you have committed a severe offence, or committed one repeatedly, it could lead to your account being suspended or having trading limits placed on it. For this reason, it's a good idea to familiarise yourself with at least the main areas of eBay policy. To view a summary list, click Customer support at the top of any eBay page, type 'rules' into the Help search box then click *Search*. Click Knowing the rules for sellers.

If you're unsure about anything, ask eBay customer support representatives for clarification.

A VeRO claim has been made against me

Verified Rights Owner (VeRO) claims can be made by a business that owns the branding and sales rights of a particular product. In this case, eBay automatically ends the listing. It is up to the eBay business to communicate with the relevant rights owner to secure permission to sell the product, or use the intellectual property, in their eBay listings. For this reason, it's essential to secure full permission from a product manufacturer to resell on eBay *before* you invest large amounts of time or capital in establishing your eBay store or acquiring stock. This is particularly important if you are selling brand-name products. Although VeRO claims are not common, it can be heartbreaking for an eBay business to be shut down because of an oversight that should have been spotted at the beginning of the planning process.

If you are the subject of a VeRO claim, communicate professionally and calmly with the rights owner. In some instances this has resulted in a profitable ongoing relationship being established. Refer back to the earlier chapters to help you create a sound business case to convince the manufacturer that their products have great sales potential on eBay. For more information click Customer support at the top of any eBay page, type 'VeRO' into the Help search box then click *Search*. Click My brand-name item was removed.

I received undeserved negative feedback

Although my professional policy is never to harass buyers over the feedback they have left, a negative feedback score and comment can feel like a real blow to any business owner. Yet receiving a negative response at some point is almost unavoidable, because eventually you will come across a buyer you simply cannot satisfy. This is particularly true for businesses with a larger number of buyers.

You can both reply to feedback left and ask for revision to feedback, but only do so when you feel it is absolutely necessary. If you are replying, keep your response factual, professional and courteous—public slanging matches are a real buyer turn-off. To reply to feedback, click Site map at the bottom of any eBay page; under the Feedback column on the right-click Reply to feedback received.

In the same location, click Request feedback revision to ask your buyer to reconsider their score and comments. Always ensure you communicate with your buyer before sending a feedback revision. Requests must be sent within 30 days of receiving the feedback and you can request revisions only five times for every thousand scores you receive per year.

Try to learn from the negative buyer comments you receive. I received one recently from a buyer who complained that the product did not perform. Had I sent a note with all packages advising that if, for any reason, buyers are unhappy they should contact me for a full refund, perhaps this could have been avoided. Taking no additional measures to avoid any type of negative feedback makes receiving it eventually almost inevitable. The truth of the matter is that occasional negative feedback is not going to send prospective buyers away in droves. Ensure you have an overall feedback score of over 99 per cent, preferably over 99.5 per cent, and avoid a string or high frequency of negative comments by ensuring all of your business operations remain highly tuned.

Running a business TOP 10

10 things you need to know about running a successful eBay business

1   Think and act like an international, progressive, multi-channel retailer—everything you do on eBay should be as good as your best competitor, anywhere in the world.

2   Think and act like an international, progressive, multi-channel retailer. (Yes, I've repeated it, just so you know how important it is!)

3   Market your eBay business. Take advantage of eBay's many built-in marketing functionalities. Never rely on your listings to draw in buyers on their own—promote your brand, your store and your eBay business at every opportunity.

4   Knowledge is power. Use all of the eBay-provided reports and create your own so you know, on any given day, how your business is performing and can quickly make changes to anything that compromises your ability to make profit.

5   Expand your business internationally without paying additional eBay fees. Your products will then be for sale both to the 7 million Australians who visit eBay each month and also to the more than 100 million active buyers across the globe.

6   Make sure your shipping provider is outstanding. This is the last experience buyers have of your business, so choose the best partner with the best services and customer relations.

7   Keep your troubleshooting tips handy—you will need to refer to them regularly.

(continued)

8 Automate leaving feedback and as much of your buyer communications as possible — remember to drive down your time overhead.

9 Use packaging that impresses your customers and keeps your products protected.

10 Choose payment options that are integrated into eBay to save you time and get your products into your customer's hands faster.

CONCLUSION

eBay is possibly the most effective marketplace the world has ever seen. Every year around 100 million buyers across the globe buy from millions of eBay sellers. I've spent 11 years working for the company and have sold more than 10 000 items. This is the third book I've written to help people discover the experience of buying and selling on eBay, because it's a business model I believe in that offers unsurpassed equality for buyers one and sellers alike. Recently eBay shares were valued at around $67 billion dollars — that's more valuable than Facebook. After more than 15 years eBay has emerged as an internet stalwart, a visionary for the future of commerce.

In this book, for the first time I've covered how best to use the site from a variety of electronic devices, including desktop computer, iPad and iPhone. eBay leads the charge on mobile commerce and its app is one of the most popular downloads in the world. In the not-too-distant future more people will be accessing eBay from mobile devices than they will from computers. Imagine the possibilities of a world where a seller's products are truly available 24 hours a day, seven days a week, 365 days a year, where sales are taking place every second of every minute. In this reality, the overheads of operating and staffing a retail store during government- or centre-imposed trading hours seem too restrictive to contemplate.

For buyers, the choice between either fighting crowds for bargains and car-parking spots, haggling with retail sales staff and searching the shelves for the right products or, as on eBay, simply entering a few search terms from the comfort of your home — or scanning barcodes wherever your mobile takes you — is becoming increasingly clear. On eBay, buyers are presented with more choice than they ever dreamed possible. The largest range of new (and used) products, many of them branded and sold at an unbeatable fixed price (not auction), from a host of professional sellers numbering in the millions in all corners of the globe is undoubtedly eBay's biggest drawcard. Put simply, there's no better place to search for a product — any product.

As eBay moves into a bright future, the company defines its global purpose as 'connected commerce'. What this means for sellers (both online and off) is that eBay will continue to bring buyers to your shop, whether that be a virtual or a physical one. As the internet's most prolific advertiser, eBay prides itself on never competing with its sellers, so when it drives traffic to its collection of sites and apps, sellers of all shapes and sizes reap the rewards.

The first thing I ever sold on eBay was a singing, dancing sunflower. Today I sold 30 products to buyers as far apart as Toowoomba and Frankston, but the experience from the first to the most recent sale has remained the same. Buyer demand is as strong today as it ever was; in fact, today there are more online shoppers than ever before. As a seller, the eBay and PayPal fees I pay are so competitive that I have not considered launching my own website.

When writing *The New eBay*, I've remained focused on you, the eBay end-user. To know eBay inside out is to have memorised a 10 000-page manual, but you don't need to do that. I recommend reading this book once from beginning to end, because getting an overview of all that eBay is capable of may inspire you in ways you never entertained. Then go back to the sections you really want to know about in greater detail, and use the index at the back to find answers to specific questions that may come up now and in the future.

eBay has a new face, a new logo and new functionality that is keeping it at the forefront of commerce. You might think you know all there is to know about buying and selling on the site, but the reality is that few of us are using the site to its full potential. This is the power of the new eBay—it delivers beyond our wildest expectations. Even now it continues to surprise me. I hope you enjoy using it as much as I do. When you next nab that incredible bargain or reach that visionary business milestone, make sure you tell your friends about it too, because the more people who use eBay regularly, the more dynamic and boundless the site will become.

You can use the internet to download any number of business plans that apply to small businesses in general. Particularly useful for Australian small businesses is the template available at the Australian Government website www.business.gov.au/businessplan. You can also download the MyBizPlan app to create your own business plan on your iPad. Business plans can be extensive, requiring many hours' work, but the more effort you put into creating a comprehensive business plan, the higher your chances of running a profitable business that has adequately planned for future challenges and growth.

Creating a strong and clear business plan is not something a lot of your eBay business competitors will have done. Investing your time up front is practically guaranteed to save you a lot more time further down the track. Don't be tempted to dive headfirst into running your eBay business. Although you may achieve sales immediately, remember that the name of the game for all business is operating at the highest profit margin over the long term.

Following is a summarised business plan that borrows heavily from the Australian Government website but incorporates eBay-specific factors you'll need to plan for. Consult a business adviser if you need additional help in completing your plan, and remember if you need to make assumptions when completing the template to be as conservative as possible to avoid inconsistencies in the future. The good news is that quite a lot of the information you include in your template can simply be cut and pasted for the creation of your business cases for potential suppliers, and even for your eBay listings and store information.

Business summary

Include as much relevant information as possible. Note that you may be able to complete the summary section only towards the end of writing your plan. Fill in more details as you gather them.

My business

- Business name
- ABN
- Business logo
- eBay user ID
- eBay store URL
- Email address
- Physical address
- Phone number
- My name
- My position
- My contact details
- Other information

The opportunity

Create a summary of what your future in this category could be like.

- The existing offline market value, local and international
- The existing online market value, local and international
- Existing eBay sales
- Number of eBay sellers
- Number of live eBay listings
- My projected eBay turnover
- My projected other turnover

Vision statement

Provide a brief three-line statement about where your business will be in three years and then in 10 years. Do not specify financial goals but be visionary: for example, 'In three/10 years I will be selling more {INSERT PRODUCT} than any other eBay seller globally'.

- Three-year vision
- 10-year aspiration

Profit statement

Provide realistic, measurable estimates for your eBay turnover in one, three, five and 10 years' time.

- Net profit in year 1

- Net profit in year 3

- Net profit in year 5

- Net profit in year 10

Operations

In this section you will outline all the people, equipment, plant and product requirements you will have in the first one to three years of operating your eBay business.

- People

  - Organisational structure
    List each person with responsibilities related to the running of your eBay business, with clear reporting lines, titles and respective responsibilities. Where no name is available, identify how you will recruit, and the salary and other employment costs.

  - My role and responsibilities
    Go into detail about what your responsibilities will be — consider including a weekly or daily breakdown of tasks and desired outcomes.

  - Training requirements
    This could include training in eBay, computer, customer service, PayPal, logistics and so on.

- Premises

  - Office requirements
    List equipment, layout, approximate costs and so on.

  - Warehousing requirements
    Include plans for layout specific to each product, equipment, insurance, costs and so on.

- Logistics requirements
  What specific requirements do staff have to pick products, package them and arrange for shipping?

- Suppliers
  List all suppliers and potential suppliers, with contact names, industry position, terms of trade and so on. Include a checklist for initial contact, meeting, presentation, agreement signed and so on.

  - Shipping
    Outline all providers and their quoted costs for distribution and so on.

  - Logistics
    Do you require any service providers to assist with logistics such as storing and packing?

  - Packaging
    List suppliers of all the packaging supplies you will require.

  - Stationery and office supplies

  - IT assistance

  - Branding and marketing

  - Legal, tax, insurance and accounting

Inventory

- Potential products
  First create a list of potential products and sources. Highlight links to sources of information that can help you provide a convincing business case for resale on eBay.

Contact name	Company name	Contact details	Product(s)	Industry information	Company information	eBay information	Meeting scheduled

- Existing inventory
  List all of the products you intend to sell on eBay, one in each column.

Product name	
Product number	
Warehouse location	
Cost	
eBay compliant?	
Re-sell rights secured?	
Average eBay sell price	

My eBay sell price	
Average shipping cost	
Average packaging cost	
eBay fees	
Payment fees	
Average net profit	
Quantity available	
Total net profit	
Supplier	
Supplier details	
Alternate suppliers	
eBay competitors	
Online competitors	
Offline competitors	

Policies

Clearly define your customer and other business policies for now and the future.

- Payment methods
  List all the payment methods you will accept and your registration information for each.

- Shipping methods
  List all of the methods you will offer and the cost of each.

- Handling time
  Outline your target for handling time.

- Returns
  Specify your returns policy.

- Customer service
  Outline your minimum service standards here, plus hours of operation and methods of contact.

- Feedback
  Specify when you will leave feedback for your buyers on eBay and your stored feedback comments.

- Warranties and guarantees
  List any additional coverage offered for your products.

Marketing

Which marketing options will you be utilising and when? Consider planning for eBay stores, email marketing, eBay Deals and Sales, advertising and so on.

	Marketing program 1	Marketing program 2	Marketing program 3	Marketing program 4	Marketing program 4
Program name					
Channel					
Target launch date					
Costs					
Target products					
Target customers					
Anticipated sales boost					

Background research

Compile all of the research you have conducted in relation to your products, the industry, suppliers, competitors, customers and eBay. Include links to relevant information, graphs, data, expert opinions and so on.

- Overall industry / category analysis

- Specific product insights

- Potential supplier insights

- Target customers
  For example, how many are there, what are their lives like, how do they shop, where do they shop?

- Online analysis
  How large is the online opportunity? You might find it easier to collect information on international online sales, as Australian data is difficult to find.

- eBay analysis
  Use Terapeak and Completed items searches to be as thorough as possible, including sellers, category information, listings, available quantities, average sell prices, links to listings, shipping methods used, payment options offered, negative feedback left.

- Competitors
  Who are they, how big are they, what are their relative strengths and weaknesses compared with yours and, most important of all, what is your experience of buying from each of the top sellers in your category?

- Potential risks/threats
  Consider new trends, entry of new players, industry risks, eBay-specific issues, updated product releases and so on.

Aspirations

This is your chance to create your dream vision for your eBay business's future. This will not only inspire you to keep driving for profitability, but may also inspire staff now and in the future. Creating clear statements and visions will also guide the formation of your brand and its personality.

- Goals
  What are the goals of your business? This is sometimes referred to as your business's vision statement: 'By 2015, my business will be …'

- Achievement milestones
  Set tasks and timelines for what is required to achieve your goals.

- Objectives
  What targets are you setting for the business? These can relate to profit, growth or service, or be industry related, for example.

Financials

- Investment
  Outline how much capital you require to get your eBay business operating, and how you will source the funds plus any interest costs and so on.

- Start-up costs
  List any one-off start-up costs required to get your business operational. Consider eBay-specific costs such as having your store professionally designed and your logo created, plus administration costs.

- Ongoing costs
  Refer to chapter 22 and ensure you include every possible cost your business will face in the course of its operation each year for the next three years. This is the only way to ascertain whether your business can generate sustainable profit in future. Create this in a table format so you can easily cut and paste into your business balance sheet or profit and loss statement.

- Profit and cash flow projections
  Work out a monthly cash flow to ensure you can meet all expected bills with projected income — remember to pay yourself, even if it's only a virtual payment. Project a point in time at which your eBay business will be truly profitable — that is, income from sales exceeds all start-up and ongoing costs.

INDEX

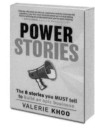

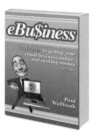